Items should be returned to
on or before the date stamped
be renewed by telep... ...or in person.

Beginner's Guide to DOS

By Dan Gookin

Edited by Gretchen Lingham and Leah Steward-Shahan
Cover illustration by Randy Verougstraete

Every effort has been made to supply the most current information regarding the software publishers and products discussed in this book. However, CPE assumes no responsibility for any infringements of patents or other rights of third parties which would result.

First Edition Copyright © 1991
Computer Publishing Enterprises
P.O. Box 23478
San Diego, CA 92193

Entire contents Copyright © 1991 by Computer Publishing Enterprises. All rights reserved. No part of this publication may be reproduced in any form or by any means, electronic or mechanical, including photocopying, recording, or by any information storage or retrieval system, without permission from the publisher.

Trademarked names appear throughout this text. Rather than provide a list of trademark holders, or use trademark symbols to denote trademarked names, the publisher and author acknowledge the trademarks and are using them for editorial purposes only. No intention of trademark infringement is intended upon any trademarked name appearing in this text.

0-945776-16-0

10 9 8 7 6 5 4 3 2

ACKNOWLEDGEMENTS

Hey! Thanks to Jack, Scott, Patti, Tina, Gretchen, Sandie and the rest of the gang at Computer Publishing Enterprises for making this book possible. Special thanks also goes to Mom, who sat down with an early draft and slugged through it like any beginner. Your help is appreciated by the author, and by every beginning DOS reader who now benefits from your suggestions.

CONTENTS

INTRODUCTION   vii

LESSON ONE: DOS and Disk

CHAPTER 1	Getting Started	3
CHAPTER 2	Working at the DOS Prompt	13
CHAPTER 3	Some Simple DOS Commands	19
CHAPTER 4	Using Your Keyboard	27
CHAPTER 5	Information, Files, and the DIR Command	37
CHAPTER 6	Files and File Contents	47
CHAPTER 7	About Your Disk Drives	53
CHAPTER 8	Formatting Disks	63
CHAPTER 9	More Fun With FORMAT	73
CHAPTER 10	Drive Logging	79

LESSON TWO: Working With Files

CHAPTER 11	Basic File Management	89
CHAPTER 12	Using the COPY Command	97
CHAPTER 13	More File Management	105

LESSON THREE: The Subdirectory Tree

CHAPTER 14	Subdirectories	115
CHAPTER 15	Working With Subdirectories	123
CHAPTER 16	File Management and Subdirectories	133
CHAPTER 17	More DIR Command Stuff	143
CHAPTER 18	Wildcards	153

LESSON FOUR: DOS Is Your Slave

CHAPTER 19	Making a Boot Disk	165
CHAPTER 20	Customizing DOS With CONFIG.SYS	171

CHAPTER 21 *Customizing DOS With
AUTOEXEC.BAT*   *175*
CHAPTER 22 *The PATH and PROMPT
Commands*   *181*
CHAPTER 23 *Using Applications*   *189*
CHAPTER 24 *Related Subjects*   *195*

APPENDICES

APPENDIX A *DOS Command Cheat Sheet*   *201*
APPENDIX B *Names*   *203*
APPENDIX C *Special Key Combinations*   *205*
APPENDIX D *PROMPT Commands*   *207*
APPENDIX E *Bits and Bytes*   *209*
APPENDIX F *Tips and Troubleshooting*   *211*
INDEX   *215*

Introduction

Welcome to *The Beginner's Guide to DOS*. This book was written to get you up and running with *DOS*, the *operating system* used by the majority of today's personal computers.

DOS is a mystifying subject. It's a stumbling block over which many beginning computer users customarily trip. It even baffles the so-called experts once in a while. So don't think you're dumb or slow for not knowing DOS. And don't be intimidated by the knowledge you're about to learn. It's important. But it's not beyond the reach of anyone who can write a check. The problem is, up until now, no one's ever bothered to *carefully* explain it.

This book will unveil the mystery of DOS, presenting it to you in a clear, easy-to-digest manner. There's no computer science degree required. No cryptic phrases to digest. No math. Everything's explained in the same relaxed manner as this paragraph. And be prepared to have some fun along the way!

THIS IS A HANDS-ON BOOK

The computer industry is big on "hands-on." It means you can touch things. Imagine walking into a swanky computer store (you know the type), and wanting to test out the keyboard on the latest machine. The persnickety salesman minces up to you and hisses, "Please don't touch the equipment." That's not hands-on.

Hands-on is grabbing. It's using your stubby little fingers to poke away at the keyboard. And in this book, it means you should have a PC and DOS all ready for your computer. You should sit in front of the computer and get ready to work. Crack your knuckles just as Bugs Bunny would before playing the piano!

People don't like to read, they like to do!

You learn by doing. More accurately, you learn by making mistakes and then realizing you've made a mistake. So be prepared to use your computer, work with DOS, and make some mistakes. Don't be afraid! There is nothing you can do here that will damage your computer—or yourself. Everything is safe and carefully explained. But your active participation is necessary.

- *And if anything important or "by the way" needs to be said, you'll see it in this format on the page.*

This book is divided into four major parts or "Lessons." You have the option of stopping between lessons, or continuing through the entire book. (Each lesson takes about two hours to do.) If you want to stop in the middle of a lesson, or even in the middle of a chapter, that's fine. The instructions for turning the PC on and off are covered in Chapter 1.

If you ever want to review information, or reference something mentioned "somewhere" in the book, turn to the Appendices. This book has a number of useful appendices, which reference all the material covered here. As a suggestion, consider ripping out Appendix A, the "DOS Cheat Sheet," and taping it up next to your computer.

GETTING STARTED

I'm going to make the assumption that you've already purchased a personal computer and know a little bit about what you bought. For example, I'm going to assume that your PC has a *hard drive* and that DOS is installed on that hard drive. If you don't, follow the instructions in your DOS manual to get DOS installed on your PC.

> ■ *If you haven't already bought a computer, then consider picking up the book* How to Understand and Buy Computers, *also written by Dan Gookin and available through Computer Publishing Enterprises.*

If you don't have a hard drive, then you're really missing the boat. A PC without a hard drive is like a tractor trailer that hauls only one bag of groceries at a time. If you decided to save some money by not buying a hard disk with your PC, then you've made a mistake. My advice: have your system upgraded with a hard disk.

You'll also need a new box of diskettes for this book. Make sure they're the proper size and *capacity* for your computer. As with a hard drive, you should have gotten a box of diskettes when you first bought your PC. If not, a call to the dealer is in order.

Finally, this book makes use of a printer hooked up to your PC. Make sure you have one, the proper cables, a manual, and some paper to print on.

VERSIONS OF DOS

There are many versions of DOS, some called PC-DOS and others called MS-DOS and still others sharing the name of your computer brand. This book calls them all just "DOS."

Version numbers are another thing. The exercises and examples in this book will work on all versions of DOS. But version 3.3 is the most reliable and I recommend it. If you already have version 4.0 or 4.01, that's okay.

> ■ *If any future versions of DOS appear, such as 5.0 or later, then they'll be okay as well. At this "beginner" level, all DOS versions work more or less the same.*

DOS IS THE KEY

The personal computer is the ultimate mind tool. It doesn't think for you. It can't. But it can help make your thinking easier. Consider it a tool for your brain like a saw or hammer is a tool for your hand. But in order to get your computer and brain connected, you need to know DOS.

DOS is the key to using a PC. You really can't avoid it—and you shouldn't. You need to know about the thing you're using before you can use it. Sure, you don't need to know the physics of internal combustion to use a car. But you need to know how to operate the car. DOS is a computer *operating* system. It sets up the rules for using your computer. You should know how to use it if you ever expect to get the most from your PC.

LOOK AT THIS STUFF

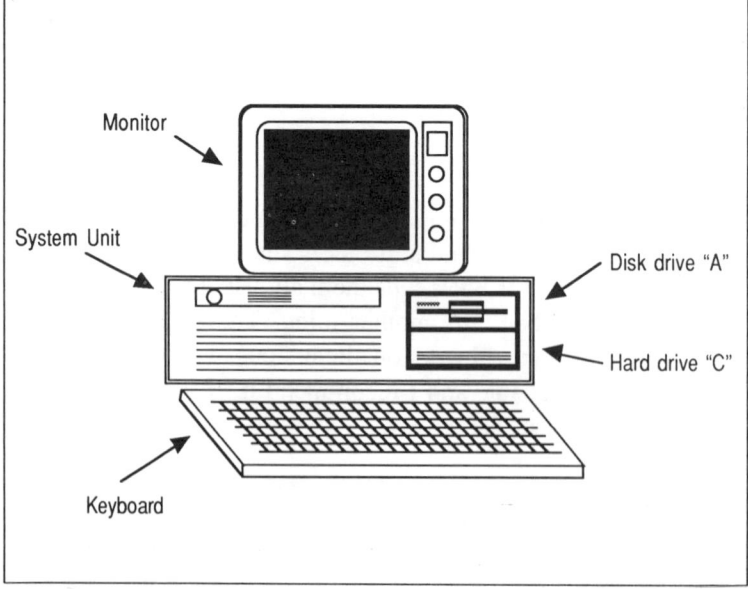

Figure 0.1: PC Map

Lesson One

DOS and Disk

CHAPTER 1

Getting Started

Perhaps the most traumatic part of daily human existence is getting up in the morning. The same thing may also hold true for a computer. (Though until the computers talk, we won't really know if it's traumatic or not.) But unlike their human friends, a computer's day starts when you turn on the power switch.

This chapter covers the starting of your computer: how you, DOS, and the PC all start working once you throw the power switch. This is the first step to beginning DOS: turning on the computer so that you can use DOS. The chapter ends with instructions on shutting the computer off. Together, these are the two extremely basic things you'll be doing with your computer.

POWER UP!

Your computer should be all plugged in, set up, and ready to go according to any directions that came with it. There should be ample instructions that tell you what to plug into what, how all the cables go, and to remind you to plug it into the wall. Don't worry about it being a mess; there isn't a computer invented that doesn't have that octopus of cables around back.

The process of powering up goes something like this:

1. Turn on all necessary *peripherals*
2. Turn on the computer

3. Enter the date and time
4. Start working with DOS

In the old days, a pre-step two was needed: Insert a *boot disk*. But with today's *hard drives*, all internally installed and permanent, that's now an unnecessary step.

Those four, basic steps are all covered right here in this chapter. Since starting the PC is something you'll probably be doing every day, these steps will be second nature to you in no time. For now, follow along closely.

Turn On All Necessary Peripherals

Get ready to start your computer by first turning on everything connected to it. Usually, this will only include the monitor. However, if you have and anticipate using a modem, printer, or any other device with your computer, turn it on as well.

The last thing you'll be turning on is the computer—the system unit—itself.

Booting

The process of turning on a computer is called booting. It's where you turn on a computer and all its peripherals (the monitor, printer, and any other devices you have hooked up to the PC).

The term booting comes from the old phrase, "pulling up your boot straps." Contrary to what some may have hoped, "booting a PC" in no way refers to kicking the machine.

For the non-boot-wearing feet out there, boot straps are little loops on the sides of a boot that help you pull the boot on. Programmers have applied the same term to the set of programming routines that start a computer. Therefore, we have the phrase "boot your computer."

Note also that booting can refer to a reset of the computer as well.

Getting Started

- *The idea here is to turn on all devices around the computer first, and then the computer itself; work from the outside in.*

An easy way to do this entire operation all at once is by purchasing a power strip or some type of "peripheral controller." For example, I plug all my peripherals and the computer itself into something called a "Power Director." I turn on the whole kit-n-caboodle with a press of one button. (These power strip-like devices also alleviate the "Vanishing Wall Socket Phenomena" computer owners experience.)

Turn On the Computer

Now you're ready to turn on your computer. Without yet doing so, here's a summary of what will happen:

First, the computer comes to life as you hear its internal cooling fan warble up to speed. The fan keeps the PC cool by drawing in air from the front of the system unit, and then forcing it out through an exhaust hole in back. Because of this, make sure the computer isn't butt-against the wall; give it some breathing room.

Second, the computer will display a message on the screen, usually a brand name or copyright notice. For example:

```
Phoenix ROM BIOS Version 3.11
Copyright (c) 1984-1990 Phoenix
Technologies
All Rights Reserved
Mondo Turbo PC Deluxe
```

Most of the newer computers will display a message like this. Some of the older models may not display anything (so don't panic if you don't see anything).

Third, nothing will happen. Don't be alarmed. During this time, the computer is performing an intensive inventory of its internal parts, as well as a self-test. Part of the self-test is a memory check, which you may see displayed on the screen as a "RAM Test" or a series of numbers that increase in size.

- *If any memory is bad, or if any part of the system fails any test, a message is displayed. When that happens, note the message and contact your dealer for service.*

Fourth, once the testing and memory count is done, your computer will beep once. That's the PC's way of saying "Hey! I'm okay." Any other beeping noise will usually signal some sort of error. (But that's rare.)

Fifth, after the beep, your PC's drive A will be accessed. Its light will come on briefly. What's happening is the startup programs built into the PC are scanning your disk drives, looking for DOS. First checked is drive A, which is followed by a check of your hard drive.

Finally, on the hard drive, the computer will find DOS. It then loads DOS into its memory and runs DOS as a program. This amazes some people: DOS is really a program—software. And it has to be loaded from disk, which is why the PC will scan for DOS on both the floppy drive A and then the hard drive when it boots.

All these steps are part of the computer's built-in instructions, part of what's called the PC's *BIOS* or *ROM*. Your computer contains a lot of smarts all by itself—otherwise it wouldn't know what to do when you first turn it on. But DOS isn't a part of those smarts. DOS must be loaded from disk.

If DOS isn't found, then a message may be displayed, telling you to insert a DOS diskette and start over. Some computers may just sit there, displaying nothing. If either of these, or anything else weird happens, refer to your DOS manual.

In summary, there are six things the computer does when you turn it on:

1. The computer comes to life; its internal cooling warbles up to speed.
2. The computer displays a copyright-startup message.
3. A memory test and internal inventory is taken.

Getting Started

4. Beep!
5. Drive A is accessed; the computer is looking for DOS.
6. DOS is found on drive C, the hard drive, and is loaded into memory

Start your PC now. Remove any floppy diskette that might be in drive A. Keep the disk drive door latch open.

Turn on the computer's switch.

Now watch your computer boot. Keep in mind the above six steps as they happen.

ENTER THE DATE AND TIME

After the booting racket has quieted down you'll find your first encounter with DOS. As it has been since day one with most computers, DOS wants you to enter the date and time. First you're asked the date, then the time.

The following shows the date prompt you should now see on your screen. (If you do not see a date prompt, then DOS has already set the date and time for you. Skim through the rest of this chapter, up to the section "Turning the PC Off.")

```
Current date is Tue 1-01-1980
Enter new date (mm-dd-yy):
```

DOS is telling you it believes the current date to be Tuesday, January 1, 1980. On the next line, you're asked to enter the new, or current date, in the format mm-dd-yy; two digits each for the month, day, and year.

Most computers today come with built-in clocks. They keep track of the date and time automatically. But thanks to tradition, DOS continues to ask for the date and time each time you start your computer. If the date you see on your screen is correct, then press Enter. If not, enter the current date in the month-day-year format.

For example, suppose today just happens to be January 15, 1992. Then you would type:

```
01-15-92
```

If you make any mistakes, use the Backspace key to correct them. Then re-enter the date. When you're done, press the Enter key.

If you see the message "Invalid" date, then you typed in the date using an improper format. Remember: two digits each for the month, day, and year, each separated by a hyphen. Do not put a period at the end of the date. Press Enter after you type in the date.

After pressing Enter, DOS asks you to enter the current time. You'll see something displayed similar to the following:

```
Current time is 0:14:54.18
Enter new time:
```

Like everyone else in today's busy society, DOS wants to know the current time. According to DOS (in this example), it's 14 minutes after midnight, plus 54.18 seconds: 0:14:54.18. Again, DOS is assuming the current time, just as it assumed the date today is January 1, 1980.

Enter the correct time. The computer uses the 24-hour "military" format, so you must add 12 to afternoon and evening hours. Two o'clock in the afternoon becomes 14:00; 7:15 at night becomes 19:15.

You only need to enter the hours and minutes, not seconds or hundredths. For example, if it's 9:35 in the morning you can type:

```
9:35
```

If the time shown on the screen is correct, then just press Enter. Otherwise, type the current time and press Enter. Use Backspace to erase if you make any mistakes.

After entering the time, you'll see a DOS copyright notice on the screen. The PC industry is big on copyrights and trademarks. Knowing what is whose keeps a whole battalion of lawyers busy day and night. You may have already seen a copyright notice when you started the PC. Now you're looking at another one. For PC-DOS version 3.3, you'll see a copyright notice similar to the one that follows.

Getting Started

```
The IBM Personal Computer DOS
Version 3.30
   (C)Copyright International Business
      Machines Corp 1981, 1987
   (C)Copyright Microsoft Corp 1981, 1986
C>
```

Other versions of DOS will display similar notices.

Look down toward the bottom of your screen. Find the last little bit of text DOS displayed.

That final doohickey DOS shows you is "C"—the *DOS prompt*. On your screen and in the above example, the DOS prompt is the letter "C" followed by a greater-than sign. (It may look subtly different.)

- *The DOS prompt is the place where you'll be entering DOS commands and running your computer's software.*

The DOS prompt is also referred to as the *command prompt*. What it does and how it works is covered in the next chapter. For this chapter, you're all done. You've successfully—and almost effortlessly—started DOS. Figuratively speaking, you've taken your first swing at the beast with your sword.

Congratulations.

TURNING THE PC.OFF

There's no use turning something on unless you know how to turn it off as well. Remember Walt Disney's *Fantasia*? Mickey Mouse cast a spell over a broom to help him clean up ("The Sorcerer's Apprentice")—but the brooms kept replicating! He knew how to start the hex, but couldn't stop it. You know how to turn on a computer, now you're going to learn how to turn one off.

Here are the basic things to remember when you turn off your PC:

1. **Make sure you're at the DOS prompt.** A few beginners will often turn off their computer to "quit" an application. I've seen this a lot. To quit their word processor, they'll turn off the PC, then start it up again to run another program. This is referred to as "cycling the power," and a bad way to treat a sophisticated electronic device.

- *Always quit your applications, returning to the DOS prompt, before you do anything else.*

   You're presently at the DOS prompt, so this step is accomplished.

2. **Remove any floppy diskettes from the floppy drives.** Remove any diskettes from your floppy drives before you turn off the power. And always remove a diskette when the drive light is off; never remove a diskette when the light is on. There aren't any floppy diskettes in your drives presently, so this step is also accomplished.

3. **Turn off all peripherals.** This step isn't needed if you're going to turn everything off at once with a master power switch.

4. **Finally, turn off the PC.** Flip off the power switch.

That's it. Basically it's the opposite way of turning the computer on. And if you *do* need to turn it on again right away, wait about 15 seconds before doing so. The components in your PC need time to "wind down." Giving them that 15 seconds will keep them happy and make sure they last longer.

Now if we could only tell Mickey how to stop those brooms...

Leaving it On All the Time

Some PC pundits recommend that you leave your computer on all the time. I know, I'm one of them.

Getting Started

There's really no reason to turn a computer off, especially if you use it every day. Keeping the system on all the time won't hurt it, and it won't raise your electric bill. (The PC uses far less energy than the refrigerator, which is on all the time, and a lot less than some plug-in water coolers.)

Turning a PC on and off isn't bad, but it's hard on the components. When you turn the machine off, it cools. Then turning it on again heats it up. That hot-cold cycle wears down the soldering joints inside the PC, making them brittle. Over a period of a few years, it could lead to trouble.

So leave the computer on all the time if you use it a lot. And if you do so, turn off the monitor when you're going to be away from the PC for a while. Leaving a monitor on leads to "phosphore burn-in," which permanently damages the monitor. It's best to keep the PC on and monitor off if you're going to be away from it for a while.

SUMMARY

To start the computer you first turn on all the peripherals, monitor, printer, and so on, then turn on the computer itself.

The computer does several things when it first comes alive. You'll see a copyright notice on the screen, and then hear a beep. Finally, the PC will look for and load DOS from your disk drives.

The first thing DOS does is ask you for the date and time. If the correct date and time are not shown, then enter them; otherwise press Enter to accept the date and time displayed.

DOS next displays a copyright notice, and then the DOS prompt, which looks like a "C" followed by a greater-than sign.

To turn your computer off, first make sure you're at the DOS prompt. Next, remove any diskettes from the floppy drives (and wait for the light to turn off before doing so). Then, shut off any peripherals, such as a printer or modem. And finally, turn off your PC's power switch.

CHAPTER 2

Working at the DOS Prompt

The DOS prompt: feared by the computer phobic, loved by the programmer, immortalized in country western songs of old. It's not scary, but it does frighten a lot of people. Why? Because they just don't understand what's going on. So instead of staring at that cryptic combination of letters known as the DOS prompt, consider it a door. Better still, consider it a keyhole, through which you can unlock the mystery of DOS.

Okay, so there's no use in romanticizing something as boring as the DOS prompt. But this chapter will cover the subject in detail. Because the DOS prompt is where you control DOS. It's a launching pad for your programs. And it's the key to using your computer and harnessing its power.

Turn your PC on again for this chapter. Remove any floppy diskettes from drive A, then flip on the power switch. Enter the date and time when asked.

WHAT IS THE DOS PROMPT?

Those of you who went running through the aisles can now safely return to your PCs. The scary part is over. Let's take an aggressive look at the DOS prompt. Strap on your helmet and shoulder pads.

Working at the DOS Prompt

The DOS prompt is where you type DOS commands, entering those secret bits of text that tell the computer what to do.

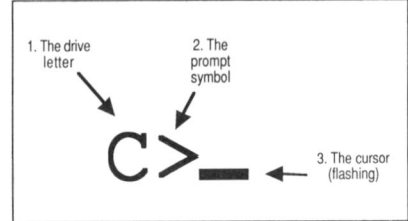

Figure 2.1. The three parts of the DOS prompt.

The DOS prompt has three parts, as shown in Figure 2.1. The first element, the "C" on your screen, is telling you that DOS is currently *logged to* drive C.

- *"Logged to" is computer jargon for "using a disk drive."*

DOS is currently using drive C, your hard drive. Therefore the "C" appears in the DOS prompt. If you were using, or logged to, another drive, then its letter would appear in the prompt. For example, "A>" for drive A.

The second element is a greater-than sign. This is simply a prompting symbol, pointing at the spot where you'll be entering your commands. It could be any other character, such as a colon or question mark, but ">" was chosen by the Powers That Be.

- *When DOS was first developed, back in the early '80s, all other computers used the ">" symbol to prompt for input. So DOS is simply being traditional —which is a pain in the neck.*

Finally, the last element is the blinking underline character next to the greater-than prompt. This is called the *cursor* and it marks the position on the screen where any characters you type will appear. At the DOS prompt, the characters will appear right after the prompt, the cursor moving to the right as you type.

USING THE DOS PROMPT

Most of your time using DOS won't be spent admiring the DOS prompt. Instead, you'll be entering commands, typing

Working at the DOS Prompt

instructions for DOS and entering the names of programs that you'll use on the computer. You send those messages to DOS via the *DOS command line*.

- *The DOS command line is the text you type at the DOS prompt.*

The cursor is blinking, anticipating your input. Let's not disappoint. Type the following at the DOS prompt—but don't press Enter.

    I LOVE MY DOS COMPUTER

You can type in upper or lower case, DOS really doesn't care. This book uses upper case throughout.

As you typed, did you notice how the cursor moved forward with you? Presently the cursor should be after the "R" in COMPUTER on the screen. See if you can find it.

You have just entered a DOS command line. This is information that you're telling DOS, a message you're sending.

Nothing is actually sent off to DOS until you press the Enter key.

- *Pressing the Enter key marks the end of input, meaning the line you just typed is okay. After pressing Enter, the command line is sent to DOS.*

By not pressing Enter you have a chance to correct your typing if you make a mistake.

For example, press the Backspace key once.

The "R" in COMPUTER is erased. As you press the Backspace key, the cursor moves to the left, gobbling up characters as it goes.

- *Backspace erases the character* before *the cursor, moving the cursor back one character position.*

Press Backspace three more times. COMPUTER has been truncated to COMPU. You could type more characters at any time. For example, type the following:

    TER

You've now restored the command line to its original state.

In practice, you'll be using Backspace to back up to a typo, correct it, then re-type the line, press Enter, and send the command to DOS.

Now press and hold down the Backspace key. Keep it down. After a moment, the entire line will be erased. Release the Backspace key.

What you've just done is to activate the *typematic* feature of the PC's keyboard. Typematic is simply a fancy term that means any key held down for a period of time automatically repeats itself. In the case of Backspace at the DOS prompt, any line you've typed will be erased. But typematic can work with other keys. If you want to lay down a line of a zillion hyphens, you just press and hold the hyphen key and, zip!, there they are.

Once again, type the following at the DOS prompt:

```
I LOVE MY DOS COMPUTER
```

This time, press Backspace to erase all the way to the space after MY. Then type in:

```
MS-DOS COMPUTER
```

The final line should read:

```
I LOVE MY MS-DOS COMPUTER
```

You could continue typing at this point, entering whatever information you like. But there is an upper limit of 127 characters (including spaces) on the DOS command line. On the screen that's about a line and a half of text. But rarely will you type that much at the DOS prompt. In fact, most command lines are only ten to 15 characters long.

Let's see what DOS thinks of your command line. Press Enter to send your command off to DOS.

```
Bad command or file name
```

DOS is telling you, and rather rudely, that it didn't understand what was just typed. Only DOS commands or the names of

Working at the DOS Prompt

programs are properly accepted. While you were probably sincere with the message, DOS just didn't understand it. (Too bad, eh?)

- *Note that nothing terrible happens when you type in a nonsense command. The computer doesn't explode and no information is lost.*

Just to prove that the computer's not biased, type in the following. Use Backspace to correct any mistakes:

```
ON THE OTHER HAND, I DON'T LIKE
MY MS-DOS COMPUTER!
```

Press Enter to see what DOS thinks of that!

A Few More Keys to Try

So far, you've used the following keys at the DOS prompt:

- Alphanumeric keys, to enter text at the DOS prompt (and the date and time)
- The Backspace key, to erase the previous character
- The Enter key, to end input and send the command line to DOS for processing

Before introducing another important key, let's see what happens when you press Enter at the DOS prompt without typing anything.

Press Enter now.

```
C>
C>
```

Pressing Enter alone does nothing. After all, you haven't told DOS anything—it just sees a blank command line.

You must tell DOS something by typing a command. If you don't like the command, you can use Backspace to erase it, but an easier way is to press another important key, the Escape key, which is labeled either "Esc" or "Escape" on your keyboard.

Type the following at the DOS prompt:

```
WHO IS SMARTER? YOU OR I?
```

You already know the answer to this question (and don't get a swelled head; the answer is "Bad command or file name"). So instead of asking it, press the Escape key.

You're screen will show:

```
C> WHO IS SMARTER? YOU OR I?\
```

Pressing Esc caused the backslash (\ ) character to be displayed. Then the cursor dropped down to the next line, under the "W" in WHO.

What you've done is to *cancel a line of input*.

- *Escape is the cancel key.*

Pressing Escape cancels the line you've just entered. DOS just ignores it. A backslash character is displayed, and the cursor drops down to the next line, once again awaiting your input. You now have the opportunity to enter a real DOS command.

Press Enter now and another DOS prompt will appear.

SUMMARY

The DOS prompt is where you enter commands for DOS and the names of programs you wish to run. Its looks are cryptic, yet they tell you the disk drive you're currently using, plus show you where your input (typing) will appear.

The text you enter at the DOS prompt, the command you type, is referred to as the "command line." To send that command line to DOS, you press the Enter key. If you make any mistakes, you press Backspace to move back and erase. Or if you want to cancel and start over, press the Escape key.

Armed with your new knowledge of using the DOS command line, it's now time to move on to the next chapter and try out some real DOS commands.

CHAPTER 3

Some Simple DOS Commands

Typing messages to DOS is fruitless. The computer is only as smart as it is. This isn't *Star Trek* where you can tell the computer to "Whip me up a chocolate malted." Things must be done according to protocol, and that requires that you enter only the names of DOS commands or programs at the DOS prompt.

This chapter is about entering real DOS commands at the prompt—meaningful command lines. Here you'll be introduced to five honest-to-goodness DOS commands that you can type in and watch work. Also covered here is the concept of internal verses external DOS commands, which will help you further understand how DOS works.

TYPES OF COMMANDS

There are two types of commands you'll enter at the DOS prompt:

- DOS commands
- Names of programs

DOS commands are instructions to DOS, directing DOS to do something, perform some action, or tell you the results of some operation or the status of another. It's basic computer-control stuff, but nothing overly technical or too difficult to deal with.

Program names are commands you give to DOS—but they aren't DOS commands; they're the names of programs on your computer. When you type a program name at the DOS prompt, DOS copies the program from disk into the computer's memory, where the program's instructions are executed.

Those are the two items you type at the DOS prompt. Actually, they're the two items that DOS understands. (As you've seen from the last chapter, you can really type anything at the DOS prompt—but what it understands isn't always what you type.)

The following sections describe some of DOS's rudimentary commands, so that you can try them out for yourself.

A Clean Slate

Take a look at your computer screen. Even though I'm not sitting there next to you, I can tell that there's a screen full of DOS prompts, a "Bad command or file name" message (or two). And other text that marks the display of any typical DOS user.

Did you notice that as you got toward the bottom of the display the screen *scrolled*? Text moved up the display, making room for new lines at the bottom. If your screen has yet to scroll, press the Enter key a few times. You'll see the text jump up, scrolling off the top.

Doesn't the screen look junky?

Type the following DOS command at the prompt:

```
CLS
```

Make sure it's typed in exactly: three letters, no period at the end, no quotes, though it can be in upper or lower case.

Now press the Enter key.

Voosh! The screen has cleared, and the DOS prompt is now on the top of a blank page (so-to-speak).

- *CLS is a DOS command that clears the screen, wiping clean the display.*

Some Simple DOS Commands   21

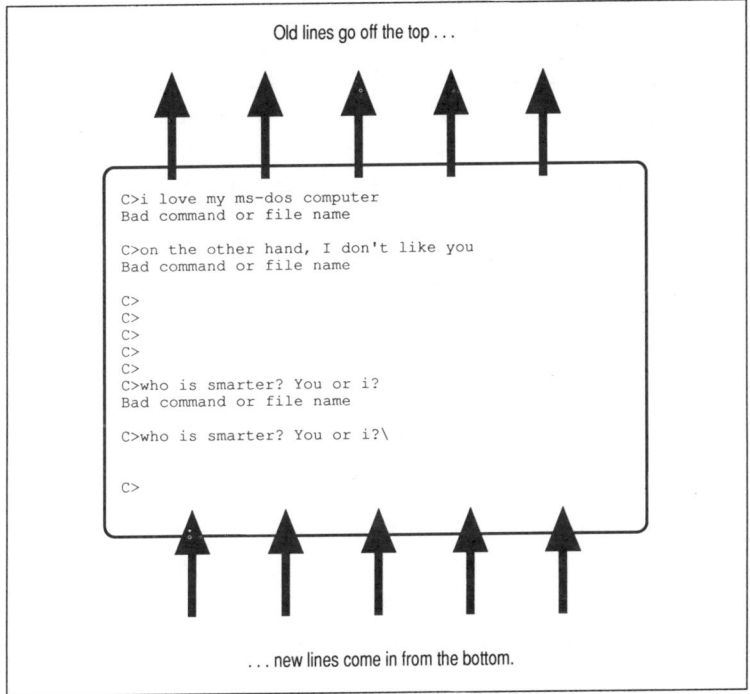

Figure 3.1 The screen scrolls.

CLS is your first DOS command. It's the clear screen command, which is where the letters CLS come from. (Pronounce it "See-El-Ess.")

You don't really need to clear your screen all the time. But it's refreshing sometimes to start over on a clean slate. Also, there are times when sensitive information may be displayed on the screen (or, more likely, an embarrassing boo-boo). In those instances, typing CLS clears the screen and your conscience. Type it again:

CLS

Press the Enter key.

Since CLS is a valid DOS command, you can type it at any DOS prompt to clear the screen.

THE DATE AND TIME

DOS likes to keep track of the date and time. It maintains an internal calendar and clock. The date and time values are used by DOS, and you'll see an example in a later chapter. Primarily, it's important to set the date and time because it lets you separate old things from recent things. This is why DOS asks for the date and time each time your computer is turned on.

Since 1985 or so, nearly all PCs come with internal, battery-backed-up clocks that always maintain the time and date. That way you only need to press Enter when asked for the time or date when the computer starts. But what if you make a mistake? Or what if you want to see what time it is right now? Or what if the battery dies?

DOS has two commands that deal with the date and time. They're called, surprisingly enough, DATE and TIME.

- *DOS's DATE command is used to set the date, and TIME is used to set the time.*

At the DOS prompt, type the following command:

```
DATE
```

Again, check your typing; it can be upper or lower case and don't follow the command with a period (DOS isn't English; you only need to press Enter to mark the end of a command).

Press the Enter key. You'll see something like the following:

```
Current date is Wed 01-15-1992
Enter new date (mm-dd-yy):
```

Deja vu! This is exactly the same prompt you saw when the computer started. However, did you notice the current date was displayed (or the date you entered when you first started the computer)? Since DOS keeps track of the date, it's always displayed when you enter, or *issue*, the DATE command.

The prompt is also there for you to enter a new date if you like. If so, remember to use the format shown. Otherwise you'll see a

Some Simple DOS Commands

message such as "Invalid date," and you'll be asked to enter the date again.

Press Enter to return to the DOS prompt, or enter a new date if you need to.

Now type the following command at the DOS prompt:

```
TIME
```

Double check your work. When it looks right, press the Enter key. You'll see another familiar prompt:

```
Current time is 1:03:52.09a
Enter new time:
```

Again, here is the time prompt, but with the current time as entered when the computer first started. As with the DATE command, you can enter a new time or just press Enter to leave it as-is.

Shortcut Alert

There are usually two ways to do everything: the long, traditional way, and a short way. With most DOS commands, there is both a long and short way. Above, you saw the long way to use the DATE and TIME commands. It goes something like this:

1. Type DATE or TIME at the DOS prompt.
2. See the current time or date (or what DOS thinks is current) displayed.
3. Optionally enter a new date or time.

Since computers were designed to save time, a shortcut for both the DATE and TIME commands exists. All you need to do is follow DATE and TIME with a new date or TIME value on the command line:

```
DATE 01-15-92
TIME 13:01
```

Experienced DOS users find this quicker than waiting for the prompt. On the downside, you're denied the benefit of seeing what DOS thinks is the current date or time.

VER AND VOL

How are VER and VOL for some cryptic computer terms? They sound like two minor characters from a Norse opera. But like CLS, DATE and TIME, they're simple DOS commands that display information on the screen.

VER

The VER command is used to display the current version of DOS. Type the following at your DOS prompt:

```
VER
```

Press Enter to send the command to DOS. You'll see the current DOS name and version displayed on your screen. Each version of DOS displays something different. PC-DOS 3.3 shows:

```
IBM Personal Computer DOS Version 3.30
```

MS-DOS 3.3 displays:

```
MS-DOS Version 3.30
```

This is exactly why the VER command is useful; it tells you which version, make and model of DOS you're using.

Okay, so you may already know that since you bought DOS with your computer. But what if you didn't? What if you're using someone else's computer and don't know which version of DOS you have? That's when you can use the VER command to find out. Also, some programs require a certain version of DOS or later. VER is a good way to verify that your DOS is compatible with that software.

■ *The differences between DOS versions, makes and models is slight. But it's something you should know.*

VOL

The VOL command is used to read the label, or name, of a diskette. This is a special electronic name given to the diskette—it's not the name you may write on the diskette's sticky-label.

Some Simple DOS Commands

In computerese, disks are referred to as *volumes*. Each disk, or volume, can be given an optional volume label name. With DOS versions 4 and later, they're also given a unique serial number.

You assign volume names to a disk using special DOS commands. But to read a disk's label, you use the VOL command.

Type the following at the DOS prompt:

```
VOL
```

Now press Enter. You should see something like:

```
Volume in drive C is DOS
Volume Serial Number is 0316-07C3
```

Above, the volume in drive C is called "DOS." If it lacked a label, then you'd see "has no label" instead of "DOS." Also, if you have DOS 3.3 or earlier, the serial number will not be displayed.

VOL's practical uses are few. DOS isn't very big on naming diskettes or using those names once you've created them. But it's a good, simple command to learn.

SUMMARY

This chapter introduced you to five simple DOS commands:

CLS is used to clear the screen.
DATE displays the date and allows you to enter a new date.
TIME displays the time, also allowing you to enter a new time.
VER displays the version of DOS you're using.
VOL displays the name, or volume label, of a disk drive.

The next chapter covers your keyboard, which is the main device you use to communicate with the computer (besides yelling at it or kicking it). Keep your computer on and ready for the next chapter.

CHAPTER 4

Using Your Keyboard

The computer talks to you via the monitor. It's the way the computer communicates with you, displaying information or results of operations. You talk to the computer via the keyboard, which is simply a glorified typewriter keyboard—but a lot quieter.

This chapter is about your computer's keyboard. It seems like a silly subject, but it's an important link between you and the PC. There are lots of keys to knowing how the keyboard works, and the secret keys it contains. Here you'll discover what those keys are, as well as read about other important keys you'll soon be using every day.

JUST YOUR TYPE

The keyboard is your line of communication with the computer. It's basically a typewriter keyboard with some extra computer-specific keys and a numeric keypad tossed in.

But the keyboard on your computer is more. In fact, it's really a computer in itself. It communicates with the main computer via the keyboard cable, sending along whatever characters you're typing and other information.

The most popular keyboard these days is the 101/102 Enhanced keyboard, which nearly every PC is now using. But there are variations. Mostly, the variations deal with the placement of a few oddball keys. Also, laptop computers will often cram in all the outside keys, lining them up like a wall around the basic typewriter keys.

- *If you're working on a laptop computer, then some of the information here, especially with regard to the numeric keypad and arrow keys, won't apply.*

Important keys to look for on your keyboard layout are Escape, marked *Esc*, and the backslash key, \ . Both of these keys are important to DOS, and their placement is non-standard.

KEYBOARD LAYOUT

There are four major areas on your keyboard. Take a look now and try to find each of the following:

- The typewriter, or alphanumeric keys
- The function keys, "F-keys," or soft keys
- Cursor control keys (only on Enhanced keyboards)
- The numeric keypad

The typewriter keys are arranged similarly to those on the IBM Selectric. The double quote key is next to Enter (called Return on a typewriter), as opposed to over the "2" key, like some systems.

You'll notice there is a Tab key and a Backspace. But there are other odd keys tossed in there: strange symbols and an assortment of brackets and braces. These symbols are used in some programs, but are found mostly in the more cryptic corners of computing. Some of them are used by DOS, and they will be mentioned as they're encountered.

Modifier Keys

In addition to the two Shift keys, there are two sets of additional "modifier" keys: a pair of Ctrl, or *control* keys; and a pair of Alt keys. (Some keyboards and laptops may only have one of

Using Your Keyboard

each.) These keys are used in combination with other keys to serve various purposes in different computer programs.

The Ctrl and Alt keys work like the Shift keys in a way: Just as you press Shift-K to get a capital "K," you would press Ctrl (control) and K to get the character *Control-K*. Pressing and holding the Alt key and K gives you Alt-K.

These Alt- and Control-key combinations are used primarily in software packages as commands. For example, you may type Alt-S to save your recipe for Wambooli punch. Or you might use Alt-P to print out a letter to your soon-to-be-former Congressman. (The function of the key depends on the software.)

Function Keys

Aside from the typewriter keys, your computer's keyboard will have function keys. Take a second to locate them now on your computer's keyboard. They could be in a single row along the top of the keyboard, or in two columns down the left side.

There are ten traditional function keys, labeled F1 through F10. Newer keyboards have F11 and F12 keys, and some keyboards go up through F16. But DOS and most software only uses the first ten.

The function keys serve a different purpose in each program you use. Some programs will have you press the F1 key to see helpful information. Others have you press F1 when you want to quit. This is why the function keys are often called "soft keys." Their function isn't preset to anything specific, but rather defined by each different program that uses them. (And that can drive you nuts at times.)

The function keys will also be used in combination with the Shift and modifier keys. For example, pressing Shift-F1, or Alt-F5, or any number of combinations is possible. This may really stretch your fingers. But it gives you up to 40 combinations of function-plus-shift keys to work with. (That's the ten function keys both alone and in combination with the Shift, Ctrl, and Alt keys.)

The Cursor Control Keys

The Enhanced keyboard has a set of ten keys snuggled between the typewriter keyboard and numeric keypad (see Figure 0.1 in the Introduction). These are special, cursor control and text editing keys, used primarily in word processing and spreadsheet software. (Older keyboards, and laptop keyboards, lack this special key arrangement.)

On top are six special keys: Insert, Home, Page Up, Delete, End, and Page Down. The latter four control what you see on the screen, and position the cursor. Insert controls the way new characters are inserted into text as you type. And Delete is used like Backspace, but deletes the character the cursor is *under*, as opposed to the previous character.

Below are four cursor, or arrow keys arranged in an "inverted T" pattern. They move the cursor in the direction they point, and are primarily used in word processing.

In DOS, these keys serve only limited functions. Before moving on, notice how the names and symbols on the keys are echoed on the numeric keypad. I'll discuss why in a moment.

The Numeric Keypad

Located on the right of the keyboard is a numeric keypad. It's the same as a ten-key pad you'd find on a calculator. In fact, many of the symbols clustered around the numeric pad are the same as you'd find on a calculator. But note that computers use an asterisk (*) instead of an "X" for multiplication.

In addition to numbers, the keypad has other symbols (arrows) and characters printed on it. These are the *cursor key controls*, used primarily in word processing and spreadsheet programs.

KEYBOARD CRYPTOGRAPHY 101

The PC's first keyboard came with an assortment of baffling symbols—not characters, but mystic arrows and hieroglyphics.

Using Your Keyboard

Most modern keyboards have labels for things such as Backspace, Tab, and Enter. But the early models—no way.

Figure 4.1 lists some of the weird arrows you may find on your keyboard, either in combination or in lieu of verbal descriptions.

Additionally, many users are baffled by the array of peculiarly named keys. Rather than slap on another curlicue, these keys have names such as PrtSc, Break, or PgUp. Relax. Everything is explained here.

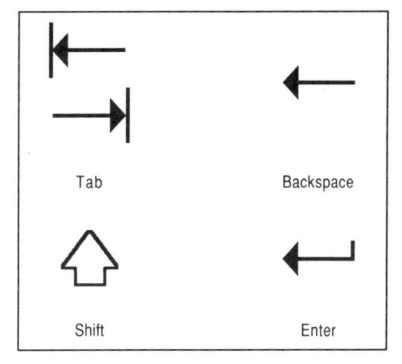

Figure 4.1: Keyboard symbols.

The State Keys

Part of the keyboard's operation is determined by three "state" keys. They are the *Caps Lock*, *Num Lock* and *Scroll Lock* keys. Take a moment now to hunt each of them out on your keyboard.

Pressing a state key changes the behavior of some part of the keyboard. When the state key is off, the keyboard responds in one manner. Turning the state key on changes the way the keyboard responds, depending on which state key was pressed. Note that each state key is pressed once to turn it on, again to turn it off. This is known as a *toggle* in computerese.

■ *Some newer keyboards have lights corresponding to each of the state keys. When the light for a particular state key is on, then that state is active.*

The Caps Lock state key is the same as the shift-lock switch on a typewriter. With Caps Lock on, YOU'LL TYPE IN ALL UPPERCASE. But unlike a typewriter, Caps Lock doesn't shift the number or symbol keys—only the letters.

Num Lock stands for Numeric keypad Lock. It's used to activate the numeric keypad. With Num Lock off, the numeric

32 *Using Your Keyboard*

```
     NumLock ON              NumLock OFF

     ┌─┐ ┌─┐ ┌─┐          ┌────┐ ┌─┐ ┌────┐
     │7│ │8│ │9│          │Home│ │↑│ │Pg Up│
     └─┘ └─┘ └─┘          └────┘ └─┘ └────┘

     ┌─┐ ┌─┐ ┌─┐          ┌─┐   ┌─┐ ┌─┐
     │4│ │5│ │6│          │←│   │ │ │→│
     └─┘ └─┘ └─┘          └─┘   └─┘ └─┘

     ┌─┐ ┌─┐ ┌─┐          ┌───┐ ┌─┐ ┌────┐
     │1│ │2│ │3│          │End│ │↓│ │Pg Dn│
     └─┘ └─┘ └─┘          └───┘ └─┘ └────┘

     ┌───┐  ┌─┐           ┌────┐   ┌───┐
     │ 0 │  │.│           │ Ins│   │Del│
     └───┘  └─┘           └────┘   └───┘
```

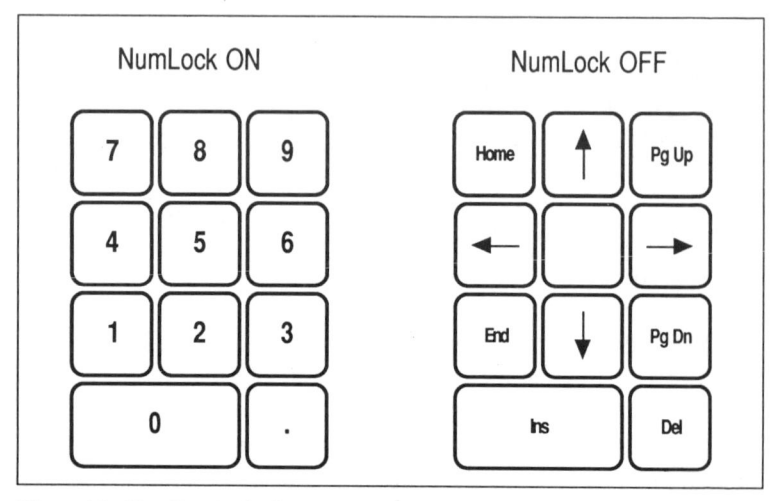

Figure 4.2: How Num Lock affects the numeric keypad.

keypad is used for cursor control. In order to activate the numbers—and "turn on" the numeric keypad—you need to switch Num Lock on. Figure 4.2 shows how the numeric keypad behaves with Num Lock either on or off.

- *The Shift key can be used to override both Caps Lock and Num Lock. For example, pressing Shift plus a letter produces a lower case letter when Caps Lock is on. Or when Num Lock is off, Shift plus a number key gives you a number.*

Finally, there's the mysterious Scroll Lock key. It's been around since day one, and a few programs use it for various purposes (mostly flight simulator games, if you can believe that). Otherwise, it's a white elephant.

SPECIAL KEYS

There are a variety of keys that serve special purposes for DOS. The following is a brief overview of the more important and useful special keys, plus a few you should pay special attention to.

Using Your Keyboard 33

- Pause

Some of the newer PC keyboards have a Pause (or Hold) key. After pressing Pause, the computer freezes, stopping in its tracks. Pressing the spacebar or Enter key will get things moving again.

Pause comes in handy when you're viewing long lists and text that scrolls off the screen. Pressing Pause freezes the action, allowing you to read the information. Then press Enter to continue, and bring the computer back to life.

Some older PCs had an invisible Pause key that was activated by pressing Shift and the Num Lock key.

- Control-S and Control-Q

In DOS you can use the Control-S and Control-Q key combinations to pause the display. Pressing Control-S pauses or "Stops" the display. Press and hold Ctrl and type an S—just as you'd type an uppercase S using the Shift key.

To continue the display, you press Control-Q, the Ctrl and Q keys.

- Print Screen

There is a key on your keyboard that will cause all text displayed on the screen to be copied to the printer. This is traditionally referred to as a *screen dump*, and it comes in handy for getting quick hard copy of information (but it only works with text—not graphics).

The Print Screen key may be labeled Print Screen, Print Scrn, PrtSc, or any combination thereof. (Some old computers just had a key titled "dump"!) If the key is Print Screen, then pressing it will give you your screen dump. The PrtSc key must be pressed with the Shift key to get a screen dump. And if you're going to try this, make sure your printer is on and has paper in it.

- Control-Break

The Control-Break key combination is the little panic button on your PC. The Break key is labeled "Break" on the front side of the key instead of the top. (It's under the Scroll Lock key on some keyboards; under the Pause key on others.) Pressing the Ctrl key in combination with Break will immediately cancel some operations on the computer. It's your way of telling the PC to "Stop!" (Hitting the Ctrl-C combination will also work under most circumstances.)

- Control-Alt-Delete

The big panic button is the Control-Alt-Delete key combination. Pressing those three keys together will totally reset your computer, starting everything over from scratch. (If your computer has a reset button, then that's a second, albeit more drastic, approach to resetting.)

- The "Any Key"

Finally, no discussion of the PC's keyboard would be complete without mentioning the Any Key.

There is no Any Key on your keyboard. Not a single key is marked with "Any." Yet, several programs will tell you to "press any key to continue." This causes some users to innocently (and vainly) scan for the Any key. A word to the wise: Any key means *any key*. But for brevity's sake, press the spacebar or Enter when they tell you to "press any key."

- *Other interesting information about the keyboard can be found in Appendix C.*

SUMMARY

The keyboard is your main line of computer control. It's divided up into four areas: the typewriter keys, the function keys, the cursor control keys, and the numeric keypad. Note that not all keyboards will have cursor control keys separate from the numeric keypad.

There are three state keys on your keyboard: Caps Lock, Num Lock, and Scroll Lock. Caps Lock is like a shift-lock on a typewriter, causing all the alphabet keys to appear in UPPERCASE.

Using Your Keyboard 35

Num Lock switches the numeric keypad from cursor control keys to number keys. Scroll lock currently doesn't do anything.

Finally, special keys and key combinations do the following:

Pause—freezes the computer, pausing the display. Press Enter or tap the Spacebar to continue.

Control-S—can also be used to pause, press Control-Q to continue.

Print Screen—is used to get a "screen dump," a copy of the characters on the screen sent to the printer.

Control-Break—is used to stop or cancel something. Control-C will also work under most circumstances.

Control-Alt-Delete—is used to reset the computer, like hitting the reset switch.

This has been more of a read chapter than a do chapter. The next chapter has more action in it than this one did. Plus you'll get a chance to try out some of these secret keyboard tricks. Keep your computer on!

CHAPTER 5

Information, Files, and the DIR Command

Using DOS means you enter commands that DOS understands. You're in charge; you tell DOS what to do. But ordering DOS around isn't the end-all of operating a computer. You do, after all, have a purpose. And that purpose involves organizing, manipulating, and using information.

This chapter takes you one level up from the "look and poke" stage of getting to know DOS. Here you're going to learn about how DOS keeps information inside the computer, and how you can view that information. This is all done via the most commonly used DOS command, DIR.

COMPUTERS AND INFORMATION

Computers are all about information. With computers, you can store and manipulate information. It's still up to you to create or gather the information, and to interpret the results. While the computer makes all the mundane parts easy for you, you're still the boss.

Information in a computer can be anything. It can be a memo, letter, report, or the first chapter in your Great American Novel. It can be a list of anyone who's ever ordered anything from your company. Information can be a list of unruly employees, people who owe you money, or religious organizations that go door-to-door.

Information, Files, and the DIR Command

DOS takes all this information and puts it on your computer's hard disk, carefully storing it so that nothing else will interfere with it and so you can get at it later.

- *The D in DOS stands for Disk. DOS is a Disk Operating System, and its primary function is to manage information on disk.*

DOS stores information in *files*. In a way, you can consider your hard disk to be a giant file cabinet. DOS's job is to take information you create or work with and keep it in separate files inside the file cabinet.

Everything on disk is a file—even DOS itself. You create files when you use software and save information to disk. DOS saves the information as a file, carefully noting its location on disk for later recall.

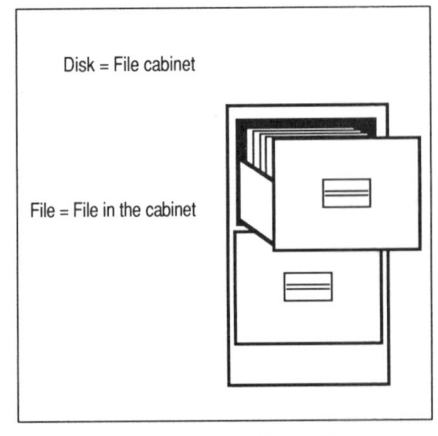

Figure 5.1: A disk is like a filing cabinet.

Everything's a file! Files are the units in which DOS stores information on disk —like sticking a sheaf of papers into a folder (the file) and then sticking it into a file cabinet (your disk drive). DOS is the file manager.

LOOKING AT FILES

DOS is happily working, putting away files you create and retrieving those you request. All the files are on disk, and DOS knows just where they are. But do you?

You can't really pry open your computer and look at the disk, fully expecting to see little files spinning around on it. Ever try looking at the recording "media" on a floppy diskette? It's black!

Information, Files, and the DIR Command

There's nothing on it to see! No writing, not even little grooves. (That's like looking at a compact disc and expecting to see written music.)

The questions arise: "How do I know what files are on disk?" "What information is already on disk?" and "How can you look to see what's there if you've forgotten?"

DOS knows. But you need to direct DOS to tell you. So you give it a command. In this case, it's the DIR command, which is short for *DIRectory*.

- *The DIR command displays a directory, or list of files on disk. This is how you locate and keep track of your files.*

Type the following at the DOS prompt:

```
DIR
```

Check your typing. Remember, you can type in upper or lower case, and don't put quotes around the command or follow it with a period. When you're ready, press the Enter key.

Every computer is different, so what you see on your screen won't be the same as what I see. (In fact, you may see quite a few lines of information scroll up your screen.) An example of something you might see is shown in Figure 5.2.

```
Volume in drive C has no label
Directory of  C:\

DOS           <DIR>         8-24-90    4:45p
AUTOEXEC BAT        128     1-15-92    9:56a
CONFIG   SYS         64     1-15-92   10:04a
COMMAND  COM      25307     3-17-87   12:00p
        3 File(s)    16140288 bytes free

C>
```

Figure 5.2: The output of the DIR command.

DIR displays a directory, or list of files on disk. Each of those files contains information, stuff that DOS has stored somewhere on the disk. You don't need to know where it is on disk; that's DOS's job. But you do need to know which files are there.

The directory listing tells you many things about your files.

40 *Information, Files, and the DIR Command*

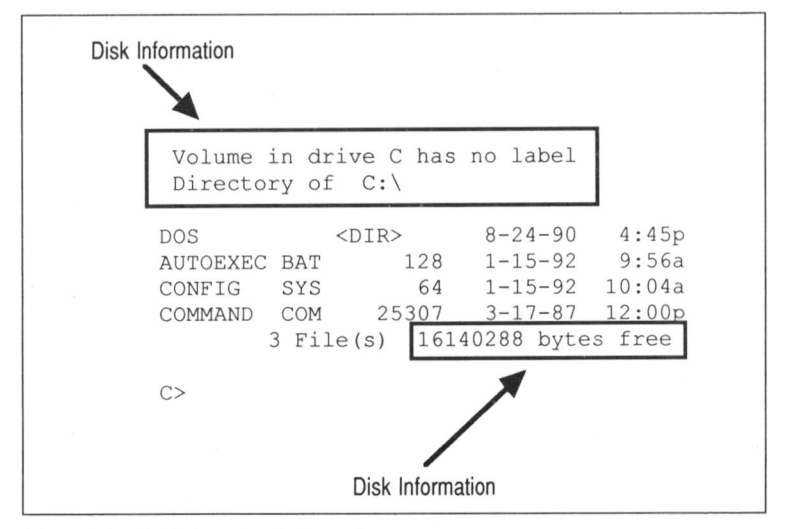

```
Disk Information

    Volume in drive C has no label
    Directory of  C:\

    DOS           <DIR>        8-24-90    4:45p
    AUTOEXEC BAT      128     1-15-92    9:56a
    CONFIG   SYS       64     1-15-92   10:04a
    COMMAND  COM    25307     3-17-87   12:00p
             3 File(s)    16140288 bytes free

    C>

                         Disk Information
```

Figure 5.3: Disk information is shown here.

Up front, it tells you the files' names—what the files are called. It also gives information about each file's size, the dates and times they were created, plus general information about the disk.

To understand the directory listing, I'm going to break it down into the following parts:

- Disk Information
- File Information
- File Name, Size, Date, and Time

Figure 5.3 shows which parts of the directory listing tell you disk information.

On top of the directory listing it tells you the disk's volume name. Deja vu with the VOL command here! The output is exactly the same. If your disk has a volume label name, it appears at the top of the listing.

The next line tells you which part of the disk contains the files you're looking at. It says "Directory of C:\." In English, this means that you're looking at a list of files on drive C. The colon following

Information, Files, and the DIR Command   41

C simply tells you that it's a drive letter, not some name. And the backslash character refers to the part of a disk where the files are located. (It's called the "root directory" and it's covered in a later chapter.)

At the bottom of the listing you see the number of "bytes free." That's the amount of bytes available on the disk drive—the remaining and unused space. (An explanation of the term *byte*, as well as *megabyte* and *"K"* is covered in Appendix E.)

If the disk drive in Figure 5.3 held a total of 20 megabytes (which is 20,971,520-or-so bytes), you would have 16,140,228 bytes available to store more information. (And using your Fourth Grade math, that means 4,831,292 bytes are currently occupied on disk.)

That's all general disk information, just bonus stuff DOS throws at you because it was thankful you asked for a directory. The remaining information deals with the files on disk—the real reason why you entered the DIR command.

Take a look at the central part of the listing on your screen. There are four columns of information.

The four columns each display different information about your files. The first one is the most important. It's the filename, what the file is called. That's how you access and identify the file under DOS. The name can be up to 12 characters long, and is divided into two parts: a name and an *extension,* (which you see as two sub-columns in Figure 5.4).

After the name comes the file's size in bytes. This tells you how fat or slim the files are. For example, in Figure 5.4, one file is only 64 bytes long, while the last one in the list is

```
Filename            Size       Date      Time

DOS              <DIR>       8-24-90    4:45p
AUTOEXEC BAT       128       1-15-92    9:56a
CONFIG   SYS        64       1-15-92   10:04a
COMMAND  COM     25307       3-17-87   12:00p
         3 File(s)
```

Figure 5.4: *Here is how information about files is displayed in a directory listing.*

25,307 bytes long. On your screen right now, locate the largest file and then the smallest file in the list.

Files can be any size, from zero bytes (which is shown by a 0 in the directory listing) to incredibly huge. One file on my disk is four megabytes in size.

- *When "<DIR>" appears in the file size column, it indicates that the file isn't a file, but rather a subdirectory. The subject of subdirectories is covered later in this chapter.*

The third column shows the date the file was created or last updated. It's shown in standard month-day-year format—just as you used with the DATE command.

The last column shows the time the file was created. It's in a 12-hour format, with a tiny "a" or "p" following the minutes to indicate a.m. or p.m. Unlike the TIME command, it's not a 24-hour format.

Finally, near the bottom you see a total of how many files were displayed. In Figure 5.4, it says "3 File(s)." Remember, a file with <DIR> by it isn't a file, but a subdirectory.

About the Filenames

In order to identify a file, you give it a name. Just about everyone names their pets, usually with a descriptive or popular name. And people sometimes name their boats, cars, and household appliances (my father does this and it drives me nuts; even the lawn mower has a name). A few people have even been known to name their children. So it is with files and information on disk.

But here comes the first of several silly limitations with DOS. It would be nice, for example, to name a file containing your July budget as "July Budget." But DOS won't let you do that. Thanks to tradition (again), DOS limits you to only 12 characters for a filename, and there can be no spaces. That doesn't leave much room to be clear or descriptive.

Information, Files, and the DIR Command

The 12 characters are further organized in what's called an *8-dot-3* pattern. Each file on disk has a primary name up to eight characters in length, followed by an optional dot (period), then up to three characters as an extension.

- *The DOS filename format is up to eight characters for the filename, followed by an optional dot and a three character extension. 8-dot-3.*

DOS lets you use all the letters in the alphabet, plus the numbers, plus a bevy of assorted symbols in a filename. A few characters are restricted. But for now, note the 8-dot-3 pattern.

Take a look at the following list of files you may see in a directory:

```
123      EXE
AUTOEXEC BAT
COMMAND  COM
READ     ME
TEST
WIN      COM
```

Above, there are six files listed. Not every one has the full eight character name, not every one has a full three character extension. One, TEST, even lacks an extension. This is all possible.

Note that the directory listing doesn't show the dot on the screen. It actually shows spaces in the filename, spaces that aren't really there (they're used to line up and format the directory listing). Yet DOS requires you to enter the dot when you type in a filename. The following shows how you would type the above six filenames if prompted:

```
123.EXE
AUTOEXEC.BAT
COMMAND.COM
READ.ME
TEST
WIN.COM
```

The dot is required if the filename has an extension. Without an extension, you don't need to type the dot, as seen with TEST above.

For now, remember the 8-dot-3 pattern and how it's displayed in the directory listing. This is background material. The remainder of this book will offer more information on filenames and extensions as it applies to the subject of each chapter.

Something Odd

The examples of directory listings in this chapter are peculiar. You may or may not have picked this up. But the total byte count of the three files listed seems rather small when you consider the total number of bytes used on the diskette. Where are the other bytes? And, if you have more files on your hard disk, and know they're there, why weren't they listed in the directory?

The answer is that not all files on your hard disk are displayed by a single DIR command. This doesn't mean you used DIR improperly, or that the command is broken.

Disks are really huge when compared to the size of the typical file. The average hard disk can hold some 40 megabytes of information. The average file is only 5K in size. This means that a typical file uses only .0125 percent or $\frac{1}{8000}$ of the total space on disk. You can pack quite a few files—thousands—on a single hard drive.

An issue with all that space is file organization. It would take you weeks to find a single file in a directory listing of some 3,000 files. What a mess!

To make things easier, disks are divided up into separate areas called *subdirectories*. Remember how the directory listing said "Directory of C:\"? The "C:\" was telling you which part, or subdirectory, on the disk you were examining. Also, you may have seen one or more items in your DIR listing with the <DIR> in the file size column. These indicate other areas on disk where more files are stored. Take a moment now to find any "<DIR>" entries you may have on your screen. Each one is a subdirectory.

Information, Files, and the DIR Command

The DIR command only lists the contents of one subdirectory at a time. This is why the byte values in the listing won't add up to the total amount of space used on the disk. Since there is probably more than one area, or subdirectory, on the disk for storing files, that explains the missing bytes (and missing files).

A later chapter on DIR, as well as chapters on the concept and workings of subdirectories, will explain how you can access those files.

SUMMARY

The subject of this chapter has been files and information, plus the DIR command used to display a list of files on disk.

Computers store information on disk in the form of files. And DOS's primary duty is as file manager, the organizer of the information and files on your system.

The DIR command is used to display a list of files on disk. The DIR command's output is formatted, and tells you lots of information in addition to the names of files. For example, some information in the DIR listing tells you the disk's volume name, total bytes, and the disk area or subdirectory you're looking at.

File information in the DIR listing displays the file's name (in two columns), the size of the file in bytes, and the date and time it was created or last updated.

Filenames under DOS use the 8-dot-3 format. You can have up to eight characters as the filename, plus an optional dot and up to three additional characters that define a filename extension.

Finally, to keep all the potentially thousands of files on your disk organized, the disk is divided up into subdirectories, each with its own group of files. When you type DIR, it only shows you the contents of one subdirectory at a time, which is why you may not have seen all the files on your hard disk with the DIR command.

Keep your computer on and ready for the next chapter.

CHAPTER 6

Files And File Contents

DOS forces you to be creative when naming a file. The 8-dot-3 format is really quite limiting. So you'll often see files such as LTR2MOM for a "letter to mom," or "JULY92" for something about July, 1992. Even so, there are still files named ZD$19BB.TGH. Who knows what that file contains!

This chapter is about files and their contents. One way to discover a file's contents is to use the *TYPE* command. TYPE is a DOS command that shows you what's in a file, and allows you to read its contents. You can also get a good idea of a file's contents by looking at its *filename extension*.

WHAT'S IN A FILE?

DOS stores information in files, and it places that information somewhere on disk. You can see a list of files via the DIR command, and you use DOS and other computer software to create and access the files. But who knows what's in them? You certainly can't tell by the underly-descriptive name.

There is a DOS command you can use to view the contents of a file: The TYPE command lists a file's contents, allowing you to see the file displayed on the screen.

- *TYPE is the DOS command that displays a file's contents.*

While TYPE is a DOS command, like VER, CLS, and DIR, it's a command that requires a *parameter*. You can't use just TYPE by itself. Instead, you must specify a filename for DOS to type. The filename follows TYPE on the command line in the following format:

```
TYPE filename
```

I don't know which files you have on disk. But chances are you have a file named COMMAND.COM. Let's take a look at it using the TYPE command. If you don't have COMMAND.COM, then use the DIR command to examine the files you have on disk, and enter one of those names instead.

Carefully type in the following command line:

```
TYPE COMMAND.COM
```

"TYPE" is the DOS command, and "COMMAND.COM" is its parameter, the file you want to display. (Don't enclose the commands in quotes; type them in exactly as listed above.)

Press Enter and watch COMMAND.COM displayed on your screen.

Oop! Eek! Ack!

- *If your computer seems out of control, beeping at you and what not, press Control-Break or Control-C. That cancels the TYPE command.*

Now you know why computers are Greek to some people. The contents of COMMAND.COM, which TYPE happily displayed for you, are not impressive. In fact, they're entirely unintelligible.

You've made no mistake. The TYPE command worked; it displayed the contents of COMMAND.COM on the screen. It's just that COMMAND.COM doesn't contain anything a human can read.

TYPE works best with text files. Those are files that contain readable text, not some computer-only odds and ends. However,

Files and File Contents 49

you can use TYPE on any file, in which case you'll see something other than text.

This all circles back to the subject of files and their contents. What's in a file?

DIFFERENT TYPES OF FILES

DOS stores all information on disk in files. But all files aren't the same. Unlike a file cabinet, where just about all the files have some sort of writing on them, humans can't read some files on disk. Most of the files, in fact, are for the computer.

Your computer can read COMMAND.COM—no sweat. In fact, COMMAND.COM is a program that's actually a part of DOS. There's nothing wrong with it, and TYPE displayed its contents on the screen. But you can't read it like you would a message. It's the wrong sort of file.

There are three general types of files on your computer:

- Program files
- Data files
- Text files

Program files contain actual instructions for the computer—programming code. DOS "runs" those programs, transferring their contents from disk into memory. DOS then points the computer's brain at the file in memory and says, "Execute these instructions here! This is a program!" And your computer runs that program.

Data files contain a variety of things, information mostly. They aren't program files, though they could be. But generally speaking, data files contain information and raw data—primarily stuff you can't read if you used the TYPE command.

Finally, *text files* are files on disk that contain text. When you use the TYPE command with a text file, you can read its contents. The text file contains words, just like you're reading now. (Text files are the same as data files, except you can read their contents.)

Making TYPE Work

The TYPE command isn't broken; COMMAND.COM was just the wrong file to look at. I chose it because I knew most everyone would have it on their system. If you have other files, as seen by the DIR command, try using TYPE with them.

- *Here's a hint: The files to TYPE will usually have an extension of BAT, TXT or DOC, though this isn't a hard-and-fast rule. See the next section.*

Use the DIR command to display a list of files again. Type the following:

```
DIR
```

Press Enter.

Look over the list of files displayed and try typing a few. For example, you may see a file called AUTOEXEC.BAT. Look through your directory listing and see if you can locate AUTOEXEC.BAT. If you find it, type in the following command:

```
TYPE AUTOEXEC.BAT
```

Press Enter to see its contents. You may not understand what's displayed, but it's a bit more readable than old COMMAND.COM.

Was there a file named "CONFIG.SYS" in the directory listing? If so, type the following at the DOS prompt:

```
TYPE CONFIG.SYS
```

Press Enter.

Look over your directory listing again. If you can't see it (it's scrolled off the screen), type in the following:

```
DIR
```

Press Enter to see the directory. Now select another file from the list. Use the TYPE command to display its contents on the screen. Enter the TYPE command, a space, then the filename just as you did above. If you don't type in the filename or TYPE command exactly, the computer will display an error:

```
File not found
```

Files and File Contents 51

You must be precise in your typing! (Though it can be in upper or lower case.) Check your spelling, and remember that a directory listing puts spaces between a filename and its extension; you must replace those spaces with a dot.

Some files are TYPE-able, others will show random "garbage." Remember, those are data and program files, which humans can't read. (And remember to press Control-Break or Control-C if the garbage overwhelms you.)

The best files to TYPE will end in TXT. Another good one is called README or READ.ME. Those files were meant to TYPE.

FILENAME EXTENSIONS

As you've seen with the TYPE command, sometimes it's impossible to tell the contents of a file by looking at its name alone. The 8-dot-3 method of naming a file just doesn't offer enough information about a file's contents.

One thing that helps is the filename extension, those optional three characters that follow the dot in a filename. Through the years, some standard filename extensions have cropped up. They can help to clue you into the file's contents, or let you know which application created the file.

For example, most word processing files end in DOC. *WordPerfect* users will sometimes end their files with WP. And plain text files commonly end in TXT. The following are some examples:

```
MEMO.DOC
MANUAL.DOC
CHAPTER1.WP
BOB803.WP
README.TXT
HELP.TXT
```

There are other semi-standards as well. Lotus *1-2-3* worksheet files end in WKS, WK1 or WK2. Database files will often end in

DBF. Graphics images may end in PIC. There are no rules, and no one "owns" any of these character combinations. But they're common enough to give you an idea about the file's contents.

DOS itself only cares about three filename extensions, and uses them to identify program files. DOS's three program filename extensions are: COM, EXE, and BAT.

- *Yes, COMMAND.COM is a program file—which is again why you can't read its contents with the TYPE command.*

If a file ends in any of these, then it's a program file. Everything else on disk would be a data file, and the data files containing readable text are text files (which you can TYPE).

SUMMARY

The DOS command introduced in this chapter was TYPE, which is used to display the contents of a file. It works like this:

```
TYPE FILENAME.EXT
```

TYPE is best used to list the contents of text files, but will display the contents of any file you specify. If you specify a non-text file, however, its contents will appear jumbled or Greek to you. (The computer will understand it just fine.)

The primary subject in this chapter was files and their contents. There are three basic types of files on your computer: program files, data files, and text files. Only the text files can be read by a human when viewed with the TYPE command. The other two types of files are only read by the computer.

You really can't tell what's in a file by looking at its limited, 8-dot-3 name. The extension helps. DOS requires all program files to end in COM, EXE or BAT. And some popular applications have their own filename extensions. These allow you to make a good guess at the file. And, of course, you can always TYPE it as a last resort to see if there's anything meaningful there.

Keep your computer warm and running for the next chapter.

CHAPTER 7

About Your Disk Drives

I've been remiss about something. For the past few chapters I've been talking about disks and disk drives, even mentioning your hard disk drive C, and haven't yet explained what it's all about. Disks are an important part of DOS (the "D" in fact). They're long-term storage, where you store your important information and your files.

This chapter is about your PC's disk drives, both the physical devices inside your computer and the diskettes they use. This is a "read" chapter as opposed the "do" chapters you've just read. But pay special attention here. The following chapter is a major "do" chapter, and it relies a lot upon what you pick up here.

DISK DRIVES

Disk drives are mechanical devices that read computer diskettes—like a tape recorder reads cassettes. A disk drive both reads from and writes to a diskette, just as you can play and record on a cassette. DOS keeps the disk drive and your PC happy and compatible.

There are two parts to a disk drive: The device itself and the disk inside. The device part spins the disk. It also controls a *read/write head*, which is the recording device that both reads and writes information from and to the diskette.

The type of disk inside the drive varies. Floppy drives use

removable diskettes. You slide them in, record on them or read from them, and then you can slide them back out, putting them away for storage. Hard drives use non-removable, "fixed" disks. You cannot take them in or out. Yet hard drives have the advantage because they store more information than floppies and can access that information quickly.

Disk Location

Disk drives are located in your computer's system unit, the main box. DOS refers to all disk drives in your system by name. But don't panic: The drives are given simple names (this isn't like memorizing "States and their Capitols"). Each disk drive in your system, from the first to the last is named after a letter in the alphabet, from A to Z.

For example, every PC has at least one floppy drive, and it's referred to as drive A. If your PC has a second drive, it's referred to as drive B.

- *Drive A is your first floppy drive.*
- *Drive B (if you have it) is your second floppy drive.*

Not every PC has a second disk drive. In fact, you only need one. Having two used to be necessary in the days of stratospheric hard drive prices. But prices have dropped, so nearly everyone now has a hard drive. And your hard drive is always referred to as drive C—even if you lack a drive B.

- *Drive C is your hard drive.*

There may also be a drive D, E, or F, depending on how many hard drives you have in your computer and how much information they can hold.

Take a second now to locate the disk drives in your system. You should have at least one floppy drive and one hard drive (which will probably be inside the computer, so assume it's there). Use Figure 7.1 to help you.

The placement of drives A and B vary from computer to

About Your Disk Drives

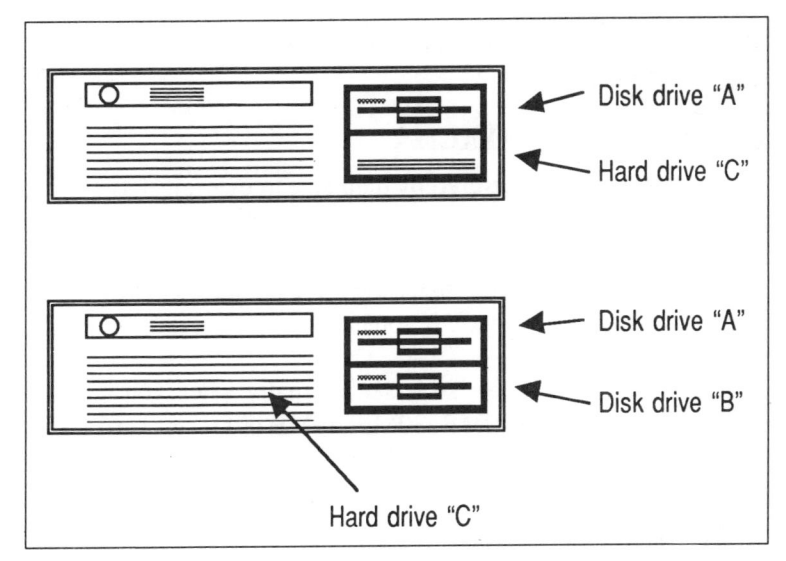

Figure 7.1: Disk drive locations.

computer. Traditionally, drive A is on top, drive B will be right underneath it. However, this doesn't always hold true—and there are no hard-and-fast rules about it. The only way to find out is to assume that A is on top. If not, the computer will let you know with a "I can't find the diskette in drive A" error.

The hard drive, C, is non-removable. Its location is fixed, either internally where you can't see it or below drive A. Since you can't remove the hard drive, or stick anything into it, its position is unimportant.

DOS refers to drives by their letter-name. But you must also add a colon when you refer to a disk drive letter:

- Drive A is A:
- Drive B is B:
- Drive C is C:

And so on. The colon is added to tell DOS you're talking about a disk drive name—not the name of a file. A, B, C, and so on are all valid, single-letter filenames. The colon causes DOS to recognize it as a disk drive.

DISK SIZES AND CAPACITY

Disk drives are measured by their size in bytes, just as trucks, ships, and in-laws are measured by their size in tons. The size is measured in *kilobytes* (K) or *megabytes* (MB). That value refers to the maximum number of bytes the drive is capable of storing on a disk. (Refer to Appendix E if you need more information on bits, bytes, K and MB.)

For hard drives, the size is set internally when you buy the drive. You can have a 20MB, 30MB, 40MB or greater hard drive. That means the non-removable disks inside the drive are capable of storing that much information—an impressive quantity.

Floppy drives are different. Their diskettes are removable. So while a single floppy drive may only be able to write 360K of information to one diskette, you could have a drawer of 1,000 or so diskettes for a potential of 360MB from one floppy drive. (But this doesn't mention all the disk swapping and shuffling you need to do to access all that information.)

Floppy drives are measured by the maximum number of bytes they can store on a single diskette. An additional measure is the physical size of the diskette they hold. Presently, personal computers use two different diskette sizes: 5¼-inch floppy disks, and 3½-inch *microfloppy* diskettes. A single drive is built to handle one or the other, not both.

- *Floppy drives come in both 5¼-inch and 3½-inch sizes.*

If your PC has one or two 5¼-inch disk drives, then that is the size of diskette you must buy and use on that system. You cannot buy or use 3½-inch diskettes—there's no place to put them! The same holds true if your system has only 3½-inch drives; you cannot use 5¼-inch diskettes. (Some PC owners do have systems with both a 5¼-inch and a 3½-inch drive.)

About Your Disk Drives

Take a second to look over your system's floppy drives to see which size they are. The 5¼-inch drives have a long, narrow slit into which you insert the diskette. They also have a door latch, which must be closed to insure the diskette is in the drive. The 3½-inch drives have a shorter slit, which is usually about ¼-inch high. Instead of a door latch, the drive will have a push button "eject" system.

Now that you know about the two different floppy drive sizes (5¼-inch and 3½-inch), let me toss you another trivia biscuit: There are also two different capacities, or *densities*, for floppy diskettes:

- Double density (or low capacity)
- High density (or high capacity)

High density diskettes hold more information than the double density diskettes. But in order to use a high density diskette, you need a high density drive for it. (Low density diskettes can be used in either drive.)

Table 7.1 will show you the amount of information you can store on each different diskette.

	5¼-inch	3½-inch
Double Density	360K	720K
High Density	1.2M	1.4M

Table 7.1: Diskettes, density, and sizes.

Remember, the diskette is closely linked to the drive. You need a drive of the same size and capacity to use a diskette to its full potential. This information only comes into play when you buy new diskettes, or when you attempt to read a high density diskette in a low density drive (which doesn't work).

Note that drive size and capacity have nothing to do with what DOS calls the drive. Drives A and B are always your first and second disk drives, no matter what their size or capacity.

58 *About Your Disk Drives*

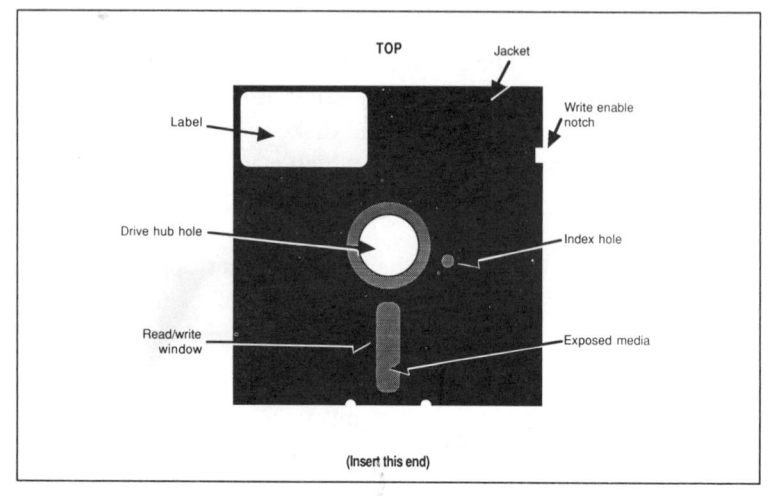

Figure 7.2: A 5¼-inch diskette.

USING FLOPPY DISKETTES

Each diskette has several parts. Figure 7.2 illustrates the major parts of a 5¼-inch floppy diskette. Figure 7.3 shows the major parts of a 3½-inch diskette.

Grab a diskette from your diskette box. Look it over and compare it with the features shown in Figures 7.2 and 7.3. For the 3½-inch diskettes, note that the lower capacity diskettes will lack the "high density media detection hole."

Here are some general diskette no-nos:

- When handling a diskette, pick it up by its top (note the top in the Figures). Keep 5¼-inch diskettes in their protective sleeve when they're not in the drive.

- Never touch any exposed media on the diskette. A thumbprint can damage the information on the diskette.

- Don't write directly on the diskettes. Write on a label first, then peel and stick it. And never pinch diskettes with paper clips or fold them or put them in the toaster.

About Your Disk Drives

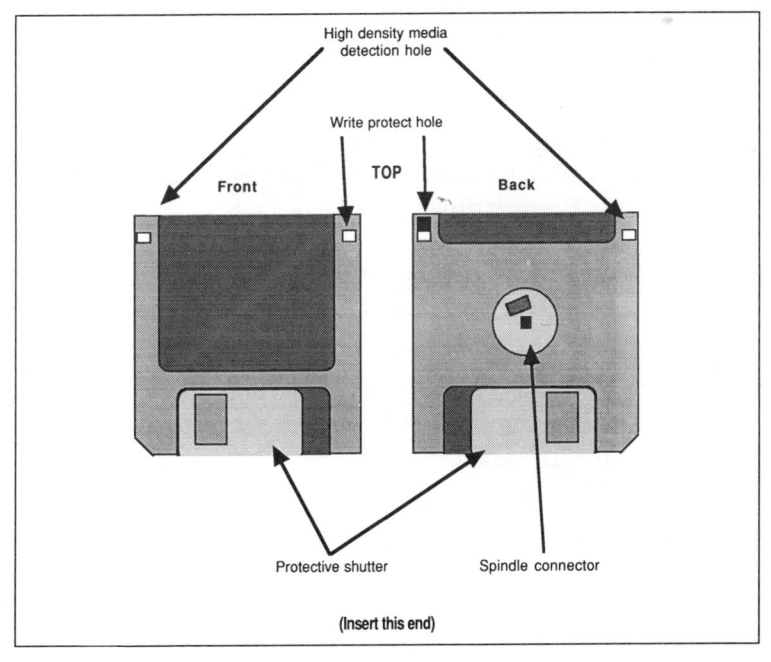

Figure 7.3: A 3½-inch diskette.

- Avoid magnets (including the one in your phone handset), direct sunlight, and peanut butter.
- Treat diskettes carefully. Sure, they're durable, but "handle with care."

Inserting a Diskette

You insert a diskette label side up, bottom edge forward. This is mainly of concern when using 5¼-inch diskettes. The 3½-inch diskettes can be inserted only one way; they just won't fit any other.

Don't worry about messing up. Everyone, from novice to old pro, has inserted a diskette incorrectly in a PC. It doesn't do any damage, but the PC can't access the diskette. Just be sure not to stick (more like wedge) a diskette *between* two drives.

Grab one of your diskettes from the box. To insert your diskette follow these steps:

1. For a 5¼-inch drive, open the drive door or latch—or make sure it's already open (it should be open, unless there's a diskette in the drive). This step is unnecessary for 3½-inch drives.
2. Insert the diskette, label side up. Slide it in all the way. Note that a 3½-inch diskette will *glide* into place. For a 5¼-inch diskette, push it in gently, as far as it goes.
3. For a 5¼-inch drive, close the drive door. If it doesn't latch properly, then the diskette is inserted incorrectly. Try again. Note that 3½-inch drives don't have a door to close. Once the diskette is in, it's in.

When the computer accesses the diskette, it spins it in the disk drive. During this operation, the tiny light on the drive will glow. That light is a warning: Do not remove this diskette!

■ *Do not remove a diskette when the drive's light is on. Even more important, do not turn off the computer when a drive's light is on.*

If you don't wait until after the light goes out before removing a diskette you may interrupt the computer as it's reading or writing information. This can really foul up the information already on the diskette.

Now remove your diskette from the drive. Follow these steps:

1. Make sure the disk drive light is off. (It should be; this is only for future reference.)
2. For a 5¼-inch diskette: Open the drive door or latch. Pinch the edge of the diskette and draw it out of the drive. For a 3½-inch diskette, press the eject button located by the drive slot. That will pop the diskette out a ways so you can remove it with your fingers.
3. Once the diskette is free from the drive, put it away.

About Your Disk Drives

Put a 5¼-inch diskette back into its envelope for safe keeping.

Always remember to label your diskettes to keep track of them. Most diskettes come with a bunch of sticky labels when you buy them. And as a tip: Write on the label *before* you stick the label on the diskette. Writing directly on a diskette, especially a 5¼-inch floppy, can dimple and damage the diskette media. (You'll be labeling diskettes in the next lesson.)

WRITE-PROTECTING DISKETTES

To protect a diskette from being written to or accidentally erased, you can *write-protect* it. Write-protecting a diskette is necessary, especially for information you don't want to accidentally lose. DOS will not update, change, or delete information on a write-protected disk. (This doesn't, however, prevent the diskette from being magnetically erased.)

The 5¼-inch diskettes use what's called a *write-protect tab*. These are tiny rectangles, often metallic, that you can peel and stick over a 5¼-inch diskette's write-enable notch. Take a moment to locate the write-protect notch on your 5¼-inch diskette. With that notch covered with one of the tabs, the diskette is "read only."

The 3½-inch diskettes have write-protect *tiles* instead of sticky tabs. To

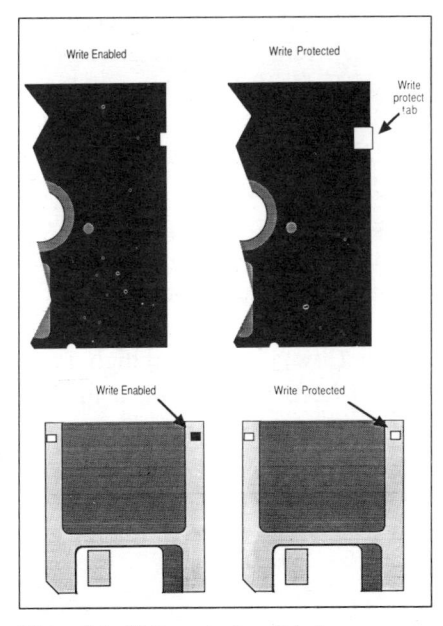

Figure 7.4: Write-protecting diskettes..

protect a diskette, you slide the tile off the hole on the diskette. If you have 3½-inch diskettes, take a moment now to locate the sliding tile. Move it back and forth: When the hole is uncovered, the diskette is write-protected. Keep the hole covered for now.

- *While you can remove the write-protect tabs from a 5¼-inch diskette, it leaves an annoying sticky residue. This is why the sliding tile on a 3½-inch diskette is such a great improvement.*

Note that hard disks cannot be write-protected. You can always write to, change, or delete information on them.

SUMMARY

Disks are one of the most important parts of your system, used for long-term storage of information and valuable files. Most PCs have two of them, a floppy disk drive A and a hard drive C. A second floppy, B, could be present as well.

DOS refers to these drives by name, but note that the letter name must be followed by a colon. The letter A alone indicates to DOS a file named "A" on disk. But A: represents your A drive.

Disk drives are measured by their capacity, the maximum number of bytes they can store. This is a fixed value for hard drives, but with a floppy drive the maximum storage depends on the drive's size, capacity, and the diskette you stick into it.

The two gauges of a floppy drive are disk size and density. The disk sizes can be 5¼-inch or 3½-inch. The densities are double (low) density and high density.

To keep the data on a diskette from being overwritten or accidentally erased you can write-protect it. This involves covering a notch on a 5¼-inch diskette or sliding the tile over the hole on a 3½-inch diskette.

CHAPTER 8

Formatting Disks

A natural follow-up to a boring chapter on diskettes and drives would be an exciting chapter on using that knowledge. Ta da! Here you have it. The subject here is formatting disks. You'll be introduced to a new DOS command, plus experience the thrill of formatting a DOS diskette—maybe more than one if the mood hits you.

For this chapter you should have a box of new diskettes handy. Make sure they match the size and capacity of your system's floppy disk drive.

ALL ABOUT FORMATTING

When you buy a box of diskettes at the store, make sure that they're 5¼- or 3½-inch—whatever size matches your drive. Further, buy either double density or high capacity, depending on what type of floppy drive you have. (The high capacity ones are more expensive in case you can't decipher the codes on the box.)

But as you're standing in line one day, this obviously Macintosh person waits in front of you. And, lo, he's buying the same sort of diskettes that you have.

What's wrong with this picture?

Nothing's wrong. Diskettes are fairly standard. They're like tube socks in a way: one size fits all. One diskette can be used by a number of different computer brands. But unlike socks, you must prepare a diskette for use with your particular computer. That's what formatting is all about.

- *Formatting prepares a diskette for use.*

As they come from the factory, all diskettes are "naked." They don't hold any information. They're blank, empty like a white canvas or like a record without any grooves. You must tell DOS that you've put a new, blank diskette into a disk drive. DOS will then prepare the diskette for use by *formatting* it just the way it likes it. The Macintosh guy will do the same thing with his diskettes. But his Mac will format those diskettes in the Macintosh way.

What Does Formatting Do?

Consider that a blank diskette is like a parking lot around a stadium. As the disk comes out of the box, the parking lot is blank—a large expanse of asphalt (minus the lamp posts). That's not very good for parking cars. Eventually, right before game time, you'd have half a billion cars wedged in there with no hope of anyone expecting to get home in time to watch highlights on TV.

So instead of having a blank parking lot, rings and rows of parking spaces are painted. Each parking space is in a row and section, which helps people to forget where they parked. This system works so well, no one but the rudest RV

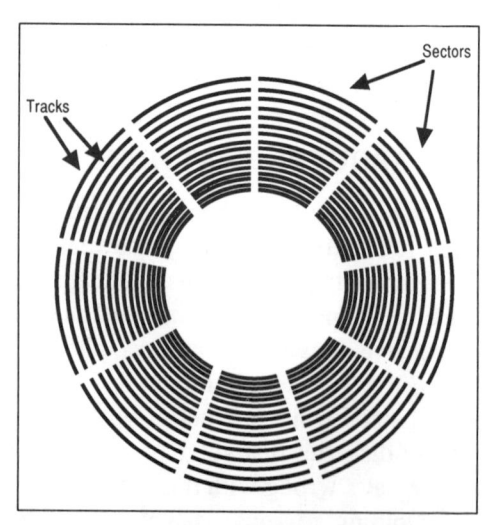

Figure 8.1: How DOS and FORMAT divide a diskette into tracks and sectors.

Formatting Disks

or Porsche owner will ignore the lines.

To prepare a disk for use, DOS formats it. This works just like painting parking lines around a stadium. In the case of formatting, DOS divides a diskette up into *tracks* and *sectors*. A track is a circle, like a circle of car slots around a stadium. A sector is a pie slice of tracks, like section A in a stadium parking lot. This is done to both sides of the diskette.

After the disk is prepared with these tracks and sectors, DOS can then place files on the disk. DOS is like the parking lot master. It puts cars into the slots and remembers where they're parked so you can get at them later. But before the files can be parked, er, saved on a diskette, it must be formatted—just like a stadium parking lot must be painted. The DOS command that does that is FORMAT.

THE FORMAT COMMAND

DOS cannot use a new diskette—no computer can. So to prepare it for use with DOS, you need to format it via the FORMAT command. FORMAT initializes diskettes, preparing them for use with DOS and your computer.

To format a new diskette, you start by inserting it into a floppy drive. Locate a new diskette and insert it into your A drive.

As with the TYPE command (Chapter 6), FORMAT requires a *parameter*. In this case, FORMAT requires that you specify the name of the drive containing the disk to format. Your new diskette is in drive A, so you would specify "A:" (remember the colon identifies a letter as a drive name). Type in the following:

```
FORMAT A:
```

Double check your typing. That's a colon after the "A" above, not a semicolon. (That's an easy mistake to make if you're typing in lower case.) Make sure the disk is properly inserted in your A drive and that the drive door is closed. Press Enter.

You should see something like the following:

```
Insert new diskette for drive A:
and press ENTER when ready...
```

Your diskette has already been inserted in the drive. Press (or "strike") Enter to begin the format.

Crunch! Hum! Spin!

DOS is now examining the diskette and preparing to format it. You can see the drive light blink on and hear the drive start to spin. What you see next depends on your version of DOS.

For DOS version 3.3, you'll see something like the following:

```
Head: 0 Cylinder: 1
```

Head and *Cylinder* refer to tracks currently being formatted. Diskettes have either 40 or 80 tracks, 40 for double density and 80 for high capacity. Head refers to the disk's sides: top and bottom. Cylinder refers to the track being formatted—those concentric circles in Figure 8.1. I agree with you if you think this is technical, but it's what DOS is telling you as the formatting progresses.

DOS versions 4.0 and later show a much friendlier percentage indicator:

```
25 percent of disk formatted
```

After a few moments (depending on the capacity of the disk), the format will be complete. For DOS version 3.3 you'll see the following:

```
Format complete
  362496 bytes total disk space
  362496 bytes available on disk
Format another (Y/N)?
```

The number of bytes on disk will change, depending on the size of the diskette formatted, which is related to the maximum capacity of the drive.

DOS version 4.0 shows you the following:

Formatting Disks

```
Format complete
Volume label (11 characters, ENTER for
  none)?
```

Press Enter for now. (We'll discuss adding the *volume label* later.) You'll see the following:

```
362496 bytes total disk space
362496 bytes available on disk
  1024 bytes in each allocation unit
   354 allocation units available
        on disk
Volume Serial Number is 193F-1CE6
Format another (Y/N)?
```

This is similar to DOS 3.3, with the addition of the allocation unit nonsense and the disk serial number (which is different for each disk). For all versions of DOS, you're asked if you want to "Format another?" You can press Y to format another diskette, or N to return to DOS.

Press N for now, then press Enter. (Remember to always press Enter after giving DOS a command.)

You're now back at the DOS prompt, and DOS is waiting for your next command. Congratulations: The diskette in drive A is now formatted and ready for you to stick files on it!

The next step is to label the diskette. Remove your formatted floppy diskette from drive A. Locate one of the sticky labels that came in the box of diskettes. Write on it, "Formatted Disk One." Then peel and carefully stick that label on the diskette.

- *You should always label all of your diskettes. Generally, you'll write something on the label that tells you about the disk's contents. Here, you're writing something that tells that diskette apart from the other, unformatted diskettes.*

If you have a B drive, try formatting a new diskette in it, as well. Follow the instructions exactly as above, substituting "B" for "A."

FORMAT will format a disk in any drive on your system, A through Z. You just specify that drive letter (and the colon) after FORMAT. But this brings up some important information about formatting drive letters C and above.

FORMAT and the Hard Drive

Drive letters of C and greater represent hard drives in your system. The typical PC has one hard drive, C. Depending on the size of the drive, it may be subdivided into a drive D and maybe E as well. (I have hard drives C through H on my system—lotsa space.) Other, high letter drives, on up through Z, could also represent hard drives on other computers via a *network*. This brings up the question, "Will FORMAT work on them as well as floppy drives?"

The answer is "yes." But . . .

Here's a good, short word of advice:

- *Do not use FORMAT on your hard drive.*

There. Wasn't that easy?

Yet, for some users, it's too easy to type in "FORMAT C:" and then . . .

Your hard drive is much too valuable for this foolishness. Sure, the FORMAT command will format your hard drive. But that effectively erases all the information you have there. Indeed, formatting any disk erases it completely. Even floppy diskettes; format a floppy disk full of files and—poof!—all that information is gone. (And DOS won't even warn you!)

If you do accidentally type "FORMAT C:" and press Enter, life doesn't come to a grinding halt. DOS will display a nice, terrifying message:

```
WARNING! ALL DATA ON NON-REMOVABLE DISK
DRIVE C WILL BE LOST
Proceed with Format (Y/N)?
```

Formatting Disks 69

Gasp! Then press N and Enter. If you press Y here, then you *will* be in trouble.

EXAMINE YOUR WORK

You should have at least one freshly formatted and labeled disk nearby. If you've removed it from the drive, stick it back in.

Let's take a look at the new diskette.

What you've done by formatting a new diskette is to create storage space for DOS and your files. Depending on the capacity of your disk drive, you now have anywhere from 360K to 1.44MB of storage available. It's in the drive, ready to work with you and your software.

"Pulling" a Directory of Drive A

To take a look at the disk, you're going to use the DIR command. After all, DIR lists the contents of a disk. (You know in advance, however, that the disk is empty and contains no files.)

- *The computer jockey jargon for looking at a list of files using the DIR command is to "pull a directory."*

The DIR command, like FORMAT, can be followed by an optional drive letter. When you do so, DIR lists the files on that drive. (When DIR isn't followed by a drive letter, it lists only the contents of the current drive.)

- *DIR can be followed by an optional drive letter, to show you the files on that drive.*

Type the following at the DOS prompt:

```
DIR A:
```

This reads, "Give me a directory of the files on drive A." Check your typing, and make sure that's a colon after "A" and not a semicolon. Press the Enter key.

Crunch! Whiz! Spin!

You should see something like the following:

```
Volume in drive A has no label
Directory of A:\
File not found
```

There are no files on drive A, which is what the above "File not found" message tells you. Other disk information is also displayed. Refer back to Chapter 5 to review what the different parts of the listing mean.

The directory listing isn't very informative. While it does explain about drive A's lack of a volume label and files, it doesn't say anything about the size of the diskette, or the available number of bytes. Still, it does confirm that the diskette in drive A is ready for use, and can be recognized by DOS.

An Experiment

Some people are skeptics. I am. You can never be too sure of something, especially all this format nonsense. Remove your formatted diskette from drive A. Now take a naked diskette from a new box and stick it into your A drive—just as you would if you were first going to format it.

Now type the following:

```
DIR A:
```

Press Enter. Here's what you should see:

```
General Failure error reading drive A
Abort, Retry, Fail?
```

This is your typical, scary DOS error message. A "general failure" in this case means that you've placed an unformatted, unprepared diskette into drive A and forced DOS to take a look at it. DOS found nothing, hence the threatening message.

The "Abort, Retry, Fail?" part of the message is a prompt telling you your options. You can press A, R, or F for the following effects:

Formatting Disks

A—Abort. Cancel the DOS command (DIR in this case), and return to the DOS prompt.

R—Retry. Remove the diskette, replace it with a good one, close the drive door, or take whatever steps are necessary (or were forgotten) to remedy the situation, and try the command (DIR) again.

F—Fail. Tell DOS to go ahead anyway—damn the disk drives, full-speed ahead! This is the worst option to select and the results are usually the same error over again, or worse. Don't press F.

Press A. This "aborts" the DOS command and returns you to the DOS prompt. You're telling DOS, "Okay, I understand. I'm sorry. I didn't *mean* to pull a directory of an unformatted diskette."

Generally speaking, always press A when you encounter the "Abort, Retry, Fail?" error message. (With DOS 4.0 and later, a fourth option "Ignore" appears; don't select it.)

Since all diskettes must be formatted eventually, why not take the opportunity now available to format the naked diskette in drive A. Type the following:

```
FORMAT A:
```

Press Enter.

Follow the instructions on the screen, or refer back to earlier in this chapter if you need additional information. (Remember to type N when it asks you to format another.) When formatting is done, remove the diskette, label it using a sticky label, and put it back into the drive.

The VOL Command (Again)

Another command that has an optional drive parameter is VOL. Remember from Chapter 3, VOL simply displays a disk's volume label, or name. To see the volume label for any drive in your system, you can follow VOL with that drive's letter (plus a colon).

Try this:

```
VOL A:
```

Check your typing, making sure you've entered exactly what's shown above (though you can type it in lower case). Press Enter. You'll see something like:

```
Volume in drive A has no label
```

Later in this book, you'll learn how to create volume labels. You can be specific, naming disks "DATA DISK" and such. But why not be cute? Imagine a volume label that shows up as follows:

```
Volume in drive A is TOO LOUD!
```

SUMMARY

This was your first real lesson in what DOS is all about. Buying and formatting diskettes is a regular part of owning a computer—no matter how much hard drive storage you have. As a good word of advice, always format a box of diskettes when you buy them; the whole box. When FORMAT asks "Format another?" press Y, remove the formatted disk and insert a new, blank one.

What formatting does is to prepare a diskette for use under DOS. It creates a series of tracks and sectors on both sides of a diskette—parking places where DOS will put your files. This is all done via the FORMAT command.

The FORMAT command must be followed by a drive letter, indicating the disk drive containing the diskette to be formatted. Drive letters range from A through Z and are followed by a colon. And though DOS can and will format drives C and above (your hard drive), don't.

FORMAT always formats a diskette out to the maximum capacity of the drive. It's possible to format a diskette of a different capacity, or to make minor adjustments in the format. This is all covered in the next chapter, which continues this discussion of FORMAT.

Keep your PC on and ready for the next chapter.

CHAPTER 9

More Fun With FORMAT

The FORMAT command is one of the most useful and powerful DOS commands. You *need* it. Even if you have an already-formatted hard drive, you'll still need to buy diskettes for backups, moving files from one PC to another, and so on. Knowing about FORMAT and using it is important.

This chapter shows you a few interesting and useful things you can do with the FORMAT command. FORMAT has many options—too many. But some of them are useful and here you'll put them to work. Also central to this chapter is the subject of a disk's volume label.

FORMAT'S OPTIONS AND SWITCHES

DOS is full of humor (at least I think so). For example, take a look at the following. Look, don't touch!

```
FORMAT drive
[/S][/B][/V:label][/8][/4][/1][/N:xx]
[/T:yy][/F:size]
```

Isn't it a scream! This is how you'll see a command listed in the DOS manual. Above is the *command format* of the FORMAT command with all possible parameters listed. (FORMAT's "optional parameters" are enclosed in square brackets; computer programmers delight themselves with being cryptic.)

You already know how to format a diskette in any disk drive: You follow the FORMAT command with the drive letter and a colon. There's nothing to it. So then, what's all that junk after the FORMAT command in our example?

Those items—that gibberish that looks like someone leaned their elbow on the keyboard—are actually *optional parameters* for FORMAT. They control the way FORMAT works, particularly what type of disk is formatted.

So the question arises, "If 'FORMAT A:' formats a diskette in drive A, why would anyone need anything else, any optional parameters, with the FORMAT command?" The answers are control and compatibility. It has to do with drive capacity, and keeping compatible with older PCs that may not have as fancy a disk drive as you do. If that issue arises, then you can customize a diskette format. Otherwise, the switches allow you to do interesting things with a diskette, such as give it a volume label.

The Volume Label

Let's put one of FORMAT's more useful switches to work. Remove any diskette that may be sitting in your A drive.

Remember VOL? Remember DIR? Both display a message such as:

```
Volume in drive A has no label.
```

Recalling from Chapter 3, a volume label is a name given to a diskette. There are two ways to do this. One is when the diskette is first formatted. The second is using DOS's LABEL command.

Locate a new, naked, unformatted diskette. Stick it into your A drive. Type the following:

```
FORMAT A: /V
```

Here, the FORMAT command is followed by the optional parameter, /V. That parameter is referred to as a *switch*. Like a light switch, it turns something on. In this case, it tells the FORMAT command to ask for a volume label when the diskette is done formatting.

More Fun With FORMAT

Press Enter. You'll see the following message:

```
Insert new diskette for drive A:
and press ENTER when ready...
```

The new diskette is in the drive. Press or strike Enter.

Let the format proceed. When it's done, DOS will display something like the following:

```
Format complete
Volume label (11 characters, ENTER for
  none)?
```

Here, DOS is asking you to enter a volume label for the diskette. You can enter a volume label up to 11 characters long. ("ENTER for none" means you can press the Enter key if you don't want the diskette to have a label.)

For the volume label, you can use letters, numbers and spaces. Lower case letters will be converted to upper case by DOS. Don't use the period, comma, quotes, or any other special characters. (There are rules about naming disks and files, which I'll get into shortly. But letters, numbers and spaces are okay here.)

Type in a volume label up to 11 characters long. (It can be less, if you like.) For example, I put the name "TEST DISK" on mine.

When you've entered your disk name, press Enter. You'll then see the rest of the information about the diskette and will be asked if you want to format another. Type N and press Enter.

Now use the VOL command on drive A. Type:

```
VOL A:
```

Press Enter. Here's what I saw on my screen:

```
Volume in drive A is TEST DISK
Volume Serial Number is 3E17-11DE
```

Your name and serial number will doubtless be different.

So What is a "Volume Label?"

There are two types of labels on a disk: the volume label, and the sticky label you apply to a diskette after it's been formatted.

More Fun With FORMAT

Remove your freshly formatted diskette from your A drive. Locate one of the sticky labels that came with your box of diskettes. Write "Test Disk" on it.

Peel and stick the label on the diskette. Now think about what's been done.

The sticky label is far more important. It tells you something about the diskette, and you don't even have to stick the diskette into the drive. (And always remember to label your diskettes.)

Later you'll be using the diskette labeled "Test Disk." When I want you to insert it into drive A, I'll just say "Insert the diskette 'Test Disk' into drive A." You'll know which diskette I mean by reading its label.

The volume label is just an electronic "name tag" you can stick on a disk. It's displayed when

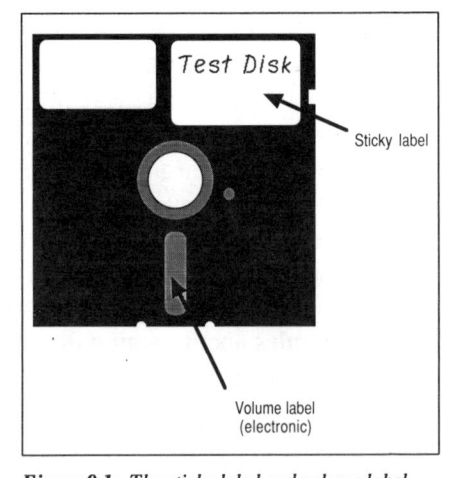

Figure 9.1: The sticky label and volume label.

you use the DIR or VOL commands—but that's about it. Few programs use it, and advanced users seldom bother with it. But for now, it's a fun thing to do and a way to learn about DOS.

The LABEL Command

Most of the time you'll be in too much of a rush to sit down and put volume labels on diskettes as you format them. I just formatted five 720K diskettes for another project. When DOS asked me to enter the volume label, I just pressed Enter (for none).

In truth, DOS and your software couldn't care less about labeling diskettes. The sticky label you put on the front of a diskette

More Fun With FORMAT

is more important than the magnetic one FORMAT applies anyway. But if you want one, and the diskette is already formatted and has valuable data, what can you do?

The answer is the LABEL command, which allows you to apply or remove a disk's volume label. (Incidentally, LABEL was only available with DOS versions 3.1 and later—DOS users had to wait 4 years to re-label diskettes!)

To rename the label on the diskette in drive A, type in the following:

```
LABEL A:
```

The LABEL command is followed by the drive letter of the disk you want to re-label. Press Enter. You'll see something like the following (but your volume label and serial number will be different):

```
Volume in drive A is TEST DISK
Volume Serial Number is 3E17-11DE
Volume label (11 characters, ENTER for
  none)?
```

There's the old label on your screen. To enter a new one, type up to 11 characters and press Enter—or just press Enter alone to erase the old label. Remember you can use letters, numbers and spaces.

If you do just press Enter alone to delete the old label you'll see the following:

```
Delete current volume label (Y/N)?
```

Press Y to delete the old label or N to keep it as is. Press Enter to get back to the DOS prompt.

If you have DOS version 4.0 or later, type the following at the DOS prompt:

```
LABEL A: DIRTY
```

Press Enter.

No feedback, eh? But try this old chestnut:

```
VOL A:
```

Better clean that disk. Get the Ajax—I'll grab a Brillo!

SUMMARY

The FORMAT command has a whole slew of options as "switches," which allow you to customize the way FORMAT formats a diskette. Most of the switches control the size of the diskette formatted. But the /V switch is used to tell FORMAT to prompt for a volume label when formatting is done:

> **FORMAT A: /V**— Formats drive A and allows for a volume label to be specified. The volume label can be seen at the top of the DIR command's output, or by using the VOL command. To change a volume label on an already-formatted diskette, the LABEL command is used.
>
> **LABEL A:**—Allows you to change the volume label for the diskette in drive A. You can enter a new label of up to 11 characters long, or press Enter alone to erase the volume label.

Keep your computer on and running for the next chapter, which is the last in this lesson. After that, you can give your computer—and yourself—a much needed break.

CHAPTER 10

Drive Logging

Put on that plaid shirt! Step outside into the great Northwest and smell the pine! It's time to go loggin'.

A-hem. Drive logging could refer to any of a number of interesting activities. For example, filling in a mileage book for tax purposes; or driving a certain number of miles on a long trip; or driving a car shaped like a giant log; etc. But the drive here is a disk drive on your computer. And logging is just another term for "using." It has nothing to do with Canada.

This chapter is about using the disk drives on your system. So far, you've only played with disk drives remotely. You've formatted a diskette in drive A, but DOS has never really "been to" drive A. To do that, you must log to drive A. This chapter tells you how to do that.

MOVING BETWEEN YOUR DRIVES

Computers have more than one disk drive. The reason is storage. Back in the old days, most PCs only had one drive—which was about all you could afford! But today, computers have at least one floppy and one hard drive.

I've skirted around the issue of using any drive at all. You know the names of the drives in your system: A, maybe a B, and

C. And when you refer to a drive under DOS, you follow that letter with a colon. But that's only half the story.

When you start your PC and it loads DOS, it loads it from the hard disk, drive C. All the time you've been using your computer, you've been using or *logged to* drive C. Even when you formatted a diskette in drive A (or B), or used the DIR or VOL commands there, you were still logged to drive C.

How do I know you were logged to drive C the whole time? Because I haven't yet told you how to log to another drive. Also, a major clue that you've always been using drive C is the DOS prompt. It reads:

```
C>
```

The "C" means you're currently logged to, or using, drive C.

Logging to Drive A

To log to another drive, you issue a DOS command. In this case, it's a guttural, grunt-and-point command; you simply type the letter of the drive you want to log to, followed by a colon.

- *To log to another drive, type its letter plus a colon at the DOS prompt. Press Enter.*

You need two things to make this happen: First, you need to know the drive's letter and second, you need to be sure that the drive is available in your system. For floppy drives, that also implies that there's a disk in the drive.

To log to drive A from drive C, type drive A's name at the DOS prompt. Make sure a formatted diskette is in drive A. Then type:

```
A:
```

Press Enter.

You're now logged to drive A. Check out the DOS prompt:

```
A>
```

Log back to drive C by typing:

Drive Logging 81

```
C:
```

Press Enter. You're now back where you started from.

Logging to Drive B

Log to drive B, your system's second floppy drive. If you have a drive B, insert the diskette you formatted back in Chapter 8.

Everybody type the following, even if your computer doesn't have a B drive:

```
B:
```

Press Enter.

You'll see the DOS prompt change from "A>" to "B>." You're now logged to drive B.

If you have a second floppy drive, this is no big deal. But if you have only one floppy drive, you might be wondering what happened. Type the following:

```
DIR
```

Press Enter to pull a directory of the diskette in drive B.

If your system doesn't have a second floppy drive, you'll see something like the following:

```
Insert diskette for drive B: and press
any key when ready
```

Press Enter. You'll now see a directory for the diskette in your B drive—but if you have only one floppy drive you see the directory for the diskette in that drive. Huh? What happened?

Logical and Physical Drives

If your system has only one floppy drive, it's referred to as *physical* drive A. That one physical drive can also be referred to as *logical* drive B. It's only one device, but by using the "logical" drive scheme, DOS can fool itself into thinking you have two drives. Even though you're still using physical drive A, DOS is referring to it as "logical" drive B.

Internally, DOS keeps track of whether your physical drive is either A or B. DOS will tell you to change diskettes between A and B if you access one or the other. This way, you can enjoy the benefits of having two drives, even if you only have one.

Log back to drive A by typing in the following:

```
A:
```

Press Enter. Now pull another directory by typing:

```
DIR
```

If you have only one floppy drive, DOS will tell you to:

```
Insert diskette for drive A: and press
any key when ready
```

Now physical drive A is once again logical drive A. Finally, log back to drive C by typing:

```
C:
```

Press Enter.

The DOS prompt should now read:

```
C>
```

Why do this? Primarily for convenience. Often you're working with multiple diskettes. To copy or move information from one to another, you could use the hard drive as an intermediate storage area. Instead, DOS allows you to use the two logical drives, A and B. That way you can copy files around, swapping diskettes as DOS tells you. DOS keeps everything straight, and in the end it's almost like having two drives.

Of course, this "practical" use is rather silly. Possibly the real reason for the "logical" drive B in a system is tradition. Again, we go back to the days of computers with only one floppy drive. In 1982 you could save $400 by not buying a B drive and DOS could still be fooled into thinking you had it. That's rather moot today—and not needed if you have two floppy drives anyway.

Drive Logging

THE MATTER OF PERSPECTIVE

Here's a new, ugly computer term for you: *default*. Yech! As with most things ugly that have to do with computers, default is a traditional term. With computers, it means "standard," "current setting," "factory selections," "whatever it is now." (In home finance, it means something nasty.)

Default is a needed term because computers are big on making assumptions. DOS needs to know the date and time. When you turn on your computer, DOS assumes the time is midnight on January 1, 1980. That's the default. Drive C is the default when you turn on the PC. It's the current drive, and many DOS commands assume you mean the current drive *by default* (or automatically).

For example, take VOL. Type the following:

```
VOL
```

Press Enter.

When you type VOL it returns the volume label of the current drive. You see "Volume in drive X . . ." where X is the current drive. Back in Chapter 3, that was drive C—and you didn't know it. The current drive was the default.

Later, in Chapter 9, you used VOL with its optional parameter, a disk drive letter. With your floppy diskette still in drive A, type the following:

```
VOL A:
```

Press Enter. The "A:" parameter caused VOL to look for a volume label in drive A. You told DOS what to do so it didn't need to assume anything.

The DIR command was the same way. DIR *pulls* a directory of files on the current drive. Unless you specify another drive letter as a parameter, DIR assumes the current drive by default.

FORMAT is an exception. FORMAT *requires* a drive letter. It doesn't assume anything. Other commands may also require you to set your parameters. But for the majority, they will assume the currently logged disk drive as the default. And other software besides DOS will have defaults and assume them as well. Keep an eye out for them.

WHAT ABOUT REAL LIFE?

Oftentimes when you're using a computer, the question of "real life" pops up. This time, the question is, "I can move between drives—so what?" How often will you be logging to another drive just to see the letter in the DOS prompt change? Rarely, if at all.

Like most tutorials, the one in this chapter was just for show. The practical, real-life part comes when you use computer programs. Specifically, when you install new software on your computer.

Normally, you'll be logged to drive C most of the time, if not all of the time. However, adding a new piece of software requires that you access drive A. That's done with:

    A:

The instructions for installing the software will often say "Log to drive A and type INSTALL." That sounds reasonable knowing what you now do. But two weeks ago it might have driven you batty. Consider what it means: "Log to drive A."

You know this means to type "A:" and press Enter at the DOS prompt. That logs you to drive A. Next you: "Type INSTALL."

This means to type the word INSTALL on the command line and press Enter. Those are the steps you should take.

Note that this is all meaningless until you've inserted the program's diskette into your A drive.

- *Make sure there is a diskette in the drive before you log to it.*

Oftentimes, computer manuals will omit that step, believing the reader to be smart enough to locate the "Installation" or "Startup" diskette and properly insert it into the correct drive. Now you know.

Drive Logging

Other instances of logging to different drives simply deal with information exchange. Nearly everyone uses hard drives. But floppy diskettes are still used for program and data file transportation. If you want to take work home, then you need to access the floppy drive, copy your work to it, and take it home.

SUMMARY

Logging to another drive is the same as using it. When you're using drive C, you're *logged to* drive C. If you want to use drive A, you *log to* drive A. This is done by typing that drive's letter followed by a colon:

A: logs you to drive A
B: logs you to drive B
C: logs you to drive C

Make sure you have a diskette in the floppy drive when you log to it. Also, if you lack a drive B, it's still possible to log to the *logical* drive B. This is actually your A drive, but internally DOS fools itself into thinking it's a drive B. You often have to switch or swap diskettes to complete the "illusion."

Shutdown

If you're the typical, budding DOS user, you've probably been sitting at your computer for a couple of hours now—or at least several action-packed minutes. It's time to stretch and take a break. But first, practice turning off the PC. To do so, follow these steps:

1. Make sure you're at the DOS prompt. (You are, so move on to step two)
2. Remove any floppy diskettes from the floppy drives. (Make sure the drive light is off before you remove the diskette.)
3. Turn off all peripherals. (Turn off your printer—if it's on—and then your PC's monitor.)

4. Finally, turn off the PC. (Flip off the power switch.)

Now get up and walk around the room a bit. Reward yourself with a trip to the refrigerator for a cool beverage and snack. You've earned it!

Lesson Two

Working With Files

CHAPTER 11

Basic File Management

File management is what DOS is all about. Everything DOS does is really to serve the file, which you remember is the basic unit of information on a disk. DOS stores files, retrieves them, runs some of them as programs, and nearly all of DOS's commands deal with files in one way or another.

This chapter is about file management. It all starts by having some files to manage, so the subject here is creating files on disk. This is done using DOS's key file manipulation command, COPY.

POWER UP

If you've turned off the computer since the last chapter, it's now time to turn it on again. To do so, follow these steps:

1. Turn on all necessary peripherals.

In this case, turn on your PC's monitor; you won't be using the printer or any other peripherals for the next few chapters.

2. Turn on the computer.

Make sure there are no floppy diskettes in the drives, then turn on the computer. (Keep all floppy diskettes out of the drive until you're told to insert them.)

3. Enter the date and time.

Use the format shown on the screen and press Enter when

you're done, or just press Enter if the correct date and time are shown.

4. Start working with DOS.
Say hello to the "C>" prompt!

FILES AND STUFF

A file is a collection of stuff on disk. The file (that stuff) gets there in one of three ways:

1. Some piece of software generates a new file
2. You use an application to create a file, say a document, worksheet, database, graphic, etc.
3. You have copied the file from an original—made a duplicate

In DOS, the COPY command is used to both generate new files and make duplicates of existing files. Since you don't already have any files to work with (at least none that I would know about), you need to create them. You'll use the COPY command to do this.

> ■ *Creating files is really a secondary function of the COPY command. Its primary purpose is to make duplicates of files already on disk. That subject is covered in the following chapter.*

CREATING FILES WITH COPY

Insert the diskette labeled "Test Disk" into your A drive. Close the drive door.

Now, log to drive A. Type in the following:

A:

Check your typing. Make sure that's a colon and not a semicolon. (Since most DOS users type in lower case, they often forget that the colon is a shift-key character.) Press Enter.

Basic File Management

You're now logged to drive A and have a fully formatted and, presently, empty diskette. (The diskette is "empty" because it contains no files.) You're ready to use COPY, not only to copy files around but to *create* files as well.

Creating ABOUT.ME

Type the following at the DOS prompt:

```
COPY CON ABOUT.ME
```

Check your typing carefully. There is a space after COPY, a space after CON, and a period between ABOUT and ME.

Press Enter.

Nothing, huh? Actually, what you've just told DOS to do is use the COPY command to create a file. DOS is copying information from the keyboard to a new file on disk. This works like a word processor, but only at a very primitive level. (I'll explain the details in a moment.)

Your job now is to type several lines of text. The file's name is "ABOUT.ME" so type a few things about yourself.

For example, for my file I'm typing the following (pressing Enter after each line):

```
Dan Gookin
Writer
P.O. Box 24296
San Diego, CA 92124
```

Here's a fun chance to type into your computer. Type a few short lines about yourself, pressing Enter after each.

Press Enter after the last line (if you haven't already done so.) Now you're ready to finish this file. Press the F6 key.

A funny symbol is displayed on your screen. It will look like this:

```
^Z
```

Find that symbol on your screen.

That doohickey is a *Control*-Z character. The caret (or hat) means "control." (You get the same result if you press the Control-Z key combination.) Why Control-Z/F6? Because DOS uses that character to mark the end of a file. In this case, you generated text for a file using the keyboard and now you're done. The Control-Z is how you tell DOS that you're done.

Press Enter. You've just made a file!

Now you see the COPY command's confirmation message:

```
1 File(s) copied
```

What You've Just Done

COPY moves information. DOS stores information in the form of files, and files are stored on disk drives. So naturally, the COPY command works with files and disk drives. But secretly, internally, COPY's job is information mover. And it moves information between DOS *devices*.

Your keyboard is a device, just like a disk drive. They keyboard's name is *CON*, for console. When you typed "COPY CON ABOUT.ME" you told DOS to read a "file" from the CON device and copy it to a file ABOUT.ME.

Since your typing at the keyboard isn't the same as a file on disk (with a definite length), you also had to tell DOS when the "file" ended. That was done by pressing F6. The F6 key generates the Control-Z character, ^Z, which DOS uses to mark the end of a file.

This is a sneaky way to create quick text files. But in real life, you'll probably use a sophisticated application, such as a word processor, to write yourself notes.

Checking Your Work

Use the DIR command to confirm that your file exists. Type in the following:

```
DIR
```

Basic File Management

Press Enter. You'll see something like the following:

```
Volume in drive A is DIRTY
Directory of A:\
ABOUT    ME        57 11-08-92 10:49a
    1 File(s)    361472 bytes free
```

The file you created appears in the directory listing. It's displayed above as the only file, "ABOUT ME" (with spaces instead of a period, which the DIR command uses to put filenames into fixed-length columns). Above, the file named "ABOUT.ME" is 57 bytes long, was created on November 8, 1992 at 10:49 in the morning.

Take a look at your directory listing's information. The information you see will reflect the file you created.

You've just created a *text file* on disk. Since a text file can be viewed and understood by humans, try out the TYPE command on it. (Remember, TYPE displays the contents of a file on disk.)

Enter the following DOS command:

```
TYPE ABOUT.ME
```

Check your typing; DOS is persnickety about spelling, spaces, and periods. When everything looks okay, press Enter. There's your file on the screen, displayed for all to see.

Making More Files

Go ahead and put a few more interesting little files on your floppy diskette. These will all be used later for more "file management practice."

How about creating a file that lists all types of food most computer people eat. Type the following at the DOS prompt:

```
COPY CON FOOD
```

Check your typing. Here, you're creating a file using the keyboard (the "CON" device) and naming it "FOOD" on disk. Press Enter.

Type in the following list, pressing Enter after each line:

```
OREOS
TWINKIES
M&MS
MALT BALLS
PIZZA
STALE DONUTS
HOT SZECHWAN
ZINGERS
```

(Add more if you like. You get the idea: computer food!)

After the last line, press the F6 key. The "^Z" appears, marking the end of the file. Press Enter, and the file is created.

```
1 File(s) copied
```

A useful file to create would be one containing some hints for DOS commands. (A complete DOS command cheat-sheet is provided in Appendix A.) Type the following at the DOS prompt:

```
COPY CON HINTS
```

Press Enter. Now enter the following lines, which should help you with some DOS commands. Remember to press Enter after each line:

```
To log to drive A, type A:
To log to drive C, type C:
To format a diskette in drive A, type
   FORMAT A:
To display a directory, type DIR
To display a directory for another
   drive, type DIR A:
To clear the screen, type CLS
To change the date, type DATE
To change the time, type TIME
To display the DOS version, type VER
To list a file's contents, use the
   TYPE command.
```

Basic File Management 95

Press the F6 key to end the file (or add more hints, if you like). Then press Enter to create it.

You should now have three files on disk. To confirm that, use the DIR command:

```
DIR
```

Press Enter and you'll see something like the following:

```
Volume in drive A is DIRTY
Directory of A:\
ABOUT    ME      57 11-08-92 10:49a
FOOD             79 11-08-92 11:02a
HINTS           395 11-08-92 11:11a
     3 File(s)   359424 bytes free
```

The three files you created are listed in the DIR command's output. They are ABOUT.ME, FOOD, and HINTS.

- *The DIR command is how you see which files are on disk. If you forget, then type DIR to see the list again.*

Use the TYPE command to view your files. Remember to follow type with the name of the file you want to view. For example, type in:

```
TYPE HINTS
```

Press Enter, and the contents of HINTS will be displayed for you.

- *The TYPE command is how you see the contents of your files on disk. Remember: DIR displays the list of files, TYPE displays their contents.*

If you'd like to create more text files, feel free to go ahead. Use the following steps:

1. Type:

```
COPY CON FILENAME
```

Replace "FILENAME" with the name of the file you want to create.

2. Enter the text of your file, pressing Enter after each line.
3. When you're done, press the F6 key, then Enter. The file is created.

SUMMARY

This chapter was your introduction to file management. The chief file management command is COPY. In this chapter, however, you used COPY to create files by copying information from the keyboard to a new file on disk.

The keyboard is the "CON" or console device according to DOS. You can copy information from the keyboard to a file using the following format:

COPY CON FILENAME

You should replace "FILENAME" above with the name of a file you want to create on disk. All text you type is then put into that file.

When you're done typing, press the F6 key. This produces a "^Z" on the screen, the Control-Z character, which tells DOS you've reached the end of the file. Pressing Enter after the Control-Z creates the file on disk.

Keep your computer on and your floppy disk in drive A for the next chapter.

CHAPTER 12

Using the COPY Command

You now have three files on your diskette in drive A, three files you created using the COPY command. But creating funny little text files isn't the COPY command's primary function (a word processor does a better job). Its real purpose is to make copies or duplicates of files—like a photocopier makes copies of documents.

This chapter is about using the COPY command to make a copy of a file. You'll be copying the files you made in the previous chapter, making duplicates of them on drive A and copying a few of them to drive C. This is the basis of all file management, and it's all really cinchy stuff.

COPYING FILES

As a review, remember that a file is a collection of stuff on disk. Files don't magically appear. Instead, they're created in one of three ways:

1. Some piece of software generates a new file.
2. You use an application to create a file.
3. You have copied the file from an original—made a duplicate.

When you tell DOS to copy a file, it looks at the original, then duplicates its contents exactly. In the end, you'll have two files that are exactly the same.

98 *Using the COPY Command*

The COPY command works like a photocopier. You put in an original, press a button, and then you have both the original and the copy. The COPY command does the same thing to a file: In the end you have both your original file and an exact duplicate—two copies of the same information.

Source and Destination

There are two terms associated with the COPY command: *source* and *destination*. They fit into the COPY command's format like this:

```
COPY source destination
```

(Of course, "source" and "destination" above would be the names of files when you use DOS.)

The source is the original file, like the sheet of paper you put in the top of a photocopier. The destination is the copy or duplicate. But in DOS, destination is actually the location of the copy—the disk drive where the copy will be located.

- *COPY is a file movement command, as well as a file duplication command. You can duplicate a file using the COPY command, but usually it's used to copy a file from one drive to another.*

The terms "source" and "destination" are used in this book. Another term, *target*, may be used instead of "destination" in some books and manuals. In that case, think of the file as an arrow that you're shooting at a target; the target is where the copy of the file will end up.

Making a Duplicate of ABOUT.ME

In its most basic form, the COPY command is used to make a duplicate of a file. Carefully type in the following:

```
COPY ABOUT.ME MYSELF
```

Press Enter. The disk drive will spin, and soon you'll see:

```
1 File(s) copied
```

Using the COPY Command

You've just made a duplicate of "ABOUT.ME" using the COPY command. The duplicate has a new name, "MYSELF." Use the DIR command to confirm that both files are on disk. Type in the following:

    DIR

Press Enter. Look for both "ABOUT.ME" and "MYSELF" in the list of files. Both should have the same size, date and time. That's one way to tell that they're identical. A second way is to list both files using the TYPE command. Type in the following:

    TYPE ABOUT.ME

Check your typing and press Enter. You'll see the contents of "ABOUT.ME" displayed.

Now TYPE the "MYSELF" file. Type in the following:

    TYPE MYSELF

Check your typing, making sure you've entered it exactly as above. Press Enter. You'll see the same contents as the "ABOUT.ME" file, which were duplicated by the COPY command and placed into the "MYSELF" file.

You can duplicate any file by using COPY in this manner:

    COPY ABOUT.ME MYSELF

Here, the source file is "ABOUT.ME" and "MYSELF" is the destination. The destination in this case isn't another disk drive, so DOS assumes you want the copy on the same disk drive. And, as you saw with the DIR command's listing, the two files are indeed both located on drive A.

But did you notice that the duplicate had a new name? This must always be the case when you copy a file on the same drive.

- *When COPYing or duplicating files on the same drive, the duplicate must have a new name.*

DOS doesn't allow two files to share the same name on a disk. It's impossible—and kind of silly when you think about it. Type in the following:

```
COPY ABOUT.ME ABOUT.ME
```

Here, the filename "ABOUT.ME" is both the source and destination. Press Enter.

```
File cannot be copied onto itself
    0 File(s) copied
```

DOS just won't let you do it.

COPYing Over a File

Pull a directory of drive A again. Type in the following:

```
DIR
```

On your screen you should see a file named "FOOD" and the file "MYSELF" is somewhere in the list as well. What would happen if you tried to make a duplicate of the file "FOOD" and you chose "MYSELF" as the name of the duplicate?

Type in the following:

```
COPY FOOD MYSELF
```

The file "FOOD" is the source and "MYSELF" is the destination. (And remember that "MYSELF" is currently a file on disk.) Press Enter.

```
1 File(s) copied
```

Hmmm. You know that "MYSELF" already exists on disk. Yet, when you used the COPY command above, it went ahead and copied a file, making a duplicate of "FOOD" and using "MYSELF" as the duplicate's name. List the contents of "MYSELF" by typing in the following:

```
TYPE MYSELF
```

Press Enter.

On your screen, you now see the contents of the "FOOD" file.

True to form, you did make a copy of the "FOOD" file using the COPY command. The duplicate file "MYSELF" was already on disk, yet the COPY command *erased* its original contents,

Using the COPY Command

overwriting it with the contents of "FOOD." The COPY command does this without warning you.

- *The COPY command will overwrite the contents of an existing file without giving you a warning that it's doing so.*

The purpose of this exercise was to show you a common mistake most DOS users make with the COPY command. Fortunately, the file "MYSELF" already contained a duplicate of another file on disk. Nothing was lost. But in the "real world," COPYing over a file means you can't get the original file's contents back. Be careful!

COPYing to Another Drive

To copy a file to another drive, you simply put that drive's letter (plus a colon) in front of the destination filename. Carefully type in the following (watch the spaces):

```
COPY FOOD C:
```

This command copies the file "FOOD" to drive C. Press Enter.

```
1 File(s) copied
```

The "FOOD" file has now been duplicated on drive C. Since you didn't specify a new destination filename, DOS assumed the source file's original name. Pull a directory of drive C to see that "FOOD" made it. Type in the following:

```
DIR C:
```

Press Enter. Look in the directory listing for the "FOOD" file.

- *When copying a file to another drive, you only need to specify the drive letter. If you do so, the copy of the file will have the same name as the original.*

The COPY command is used in this way to move files around, between your hard drive and a floppy drive. Say you wanted to take a project home from work for the home computer. You'd use COPY to copy it to a floppy diskette and then take that diskette home.

You can also specify a new name for the copy if you like. Type in the following:

COPY FOOD C:SNACKS

Here you're still copying the file "FOOD" to drive C. But the file will be given the name "SNACKS" (a more accurate name when you consider the file's contents). Double check your typing, and press Enter.

1 File(s) copied

Again, pull a directory for drive C. Type in:

DIR C:

Press Enter. Look for the two files "FOOD" and "SNACKS" in the listing. They'll both have the same contents, file size, date and time.

COPYing Without a Destination

When you make a copy of a file, all DOS really needs to know is the source filename. Under the right circumstances, DOS will assume where you want the file to go. Type in the following:

COPY C:SNACKS

Press Enter.

1 File(s) copied

To see what happened, pull a directory of drive A. Type:

DIR

Press Enter. Look for the "SNACKS" file.

If you don't specify a destination, DOS will assume that you mean the current drive as the destination. So the file "SNACKS" was copied from drive C to the current drive, A. It was also given the same name.

Earlier, you learned that the COPY command required both a source and destination. But under the proper circumstances, the destination is optional.

Using the COPY Command

- *COPY's destination file can be optional when you're copying* from *another drive* to *the current drive, in other words, when the "source" file isn't on the current drive.*

This trick (omitting a destination) only works when the source file is on another drive.

RULES FOR NAMING FILES

DOS has specific rules for naming files, and there are certain characters you cannot use in a filename. This is important because COPY and other DOS commands require you to name files. It must be done properly.

All files on disk have a name. And as you read in Chapters 5 and 6, all files are named using the 8-dot-3 pattern. That's up to eight characters for the filename, followed by an optional dot (a period) and up to three additional characters.

These "characters" in a filename consist of all the letters in the alphabet, numbers, and all other symbols on the keyboard. The only characters you cannot have in a filename are listed below:

" / \ [ ] : * | + = ; , ? < >

Add to that list the space character. Filenames cannot be broken up by spaces; they must be solid. See the table below for a comparison of valid and invalid filenames.

If you just stick with numbers and letters, and keep them in the 8-dot-3 format, you'll be safe. A common rumor is that you

Valid Filenames:	Invalid Filenames:
A	STATEMENTS—(too long)
ED	"QUOTES"—(improper characters)
TESTFILE	I.LOVE.YOU—(too many periods, extension too long)
B.1	
5-9-92	MY DIARY—(contains a space)
READ.ME	.TXT—(file lacks a filename/starts with an invalid character)
TEMP.$$$	

cannot start a filename with a number, but that's untrue. A filename can start with any allowable character, including symbols not listed in the above no-no list. (Additional information on naming files is provided in Appendix B.)

SUMMARY

The COPY command is used to make duplicates of files. You specify a source file and a destination file. The contents of the source are duplicated and placed into the destination. For example:

```
COPY FILE1 FILE2
```

Here, a new file named "FILE2" is created. It will have the same contents as the original. Note that both files will exist on the same drive, and therefore they must have different names.

You can copy a file to another drive simply by specifying the drive letter. For example:

```
COPY FILE1 C:
```

This copies the file "FILE1" to drive C. Since a new name wasn't specified, the file will also be named "FILE1" on drive C. To specify a new name, just list it after "C:" as in:

```
COPY FILE1 C:FILE2
```

Finally, you can copy a file from another drive to the current drive, simply by specifying the source:

```
COPY C:FILE1
```

Here, DOS assumes that you want to copy the file "FILE1" from drive C to the current drive. The duplicate will have the same name as the original.

One final, important note about the COPY command is that you can overwrite existing files without being warned by DOS. For example, if "FILE2" (above) already exists, DOS will overwrite it with the contents of the source file.

Keep your computer on and your floppy disk in drive A for the next chapter.

CHAPTER 13

More File Management

Files are really important tidbits of information on your computer. Soon, you'll be generating files using the software on your computer. Your word processor will produce documents, your database will produce lists of information, and other software will generate files as well. The management and upkeep of those files is done by DOS, but you must tell DOS what to do with those files. The organizational part is up to you.

This chapter continues the subject of file management. The key file manipulating command is COPY. Two other popular file commands are REN, which RENames files, and DEL, which DELetes them. This chapter will teach you how they work.

RENAMING FILES WITH REN

Make sure your diskette from the previous chapter is still in your A drive, and that you're currently logged to drive A. (Type "A:" to log to drive A if the prompt reads "C" or something else.)

You can change the name of a file without affecting the file's contents. The DOS command to do that is REN or RENAME. Yes, there are two versions of this DOS command: an abbreviated version REN, and the longer version RENAME. (Quite a few DOS commands have short and long versions.) Both commands assign a new name to a file.

■ *Most DOS users will only use the shorter version of a command. That's true in this book, where you'll see REN used instead of RENAME. Remember, both commands work the same way and do the same thing.*

Carefully type in the following:

```
REN MYSELF GOODIES
```

Press Enter.

The REN command, unlike COPY, doesn't give you any visual feedback. What's happened is that you've renamed the file "MYSELF" using "GOODIES" as its new name. (Through the course of the previous chapter, the "MYSELF" ended up with a copy of the "FOOD" file's contents.)

To verify your work, and see a list of the files on the diskette in drive A, type in the DIR command:

```
DIR
```

Press Enter.

Locate the file "GOODIES" in the list. The only thing that's changed about the file is its name. The contents of a file are unaffected by the REN command. To confirm this, list the file's contents by typing:

```
TYPE GOODIES
```

Press Enter.

If you want to rename a file on another disk drive, you must specify the drive letter and a colon before the first filename. For example, the file "SNACKS" is on your C drive. To rename it while logged to drive A, you simply specify "C:" before the filename. Carefully type in the following:

```
REN C:SNACKS GOODIES
```

Press Enter.

More File Management

The file "SNACKS" on drive C now has a new name. It was renamed "GOODIES" using the REN command. Confirm this by scanning a directory of the files on drive C. Type in the following:

```
DIR C:
```

Press Enter. Look for the file "GOODIES" in the list.

You can rename a file on any drive simply by putting the proper drive letter (and colon) in front of its name. If you don't, then DOS assumes the file is on the current drive and it will look for it there. Also, note that the drive letter is only required by the first name—the file's original name.

What happens if you rename a file using a name already on disk? Type in the following:

```
REN SNACKS FOOD
```

Both files already exist on drive A. Press Enter to see what DOS does.

```
Duplicate file name or File not found
```

DOS will not allow you to have more than one file with the same name on the same disk. The above error message confirms that. Note that you'll also see that error message if you mistype a filename. For example, if you had typed "SNAKS" (forgotten the "C"), you'd see the same message.

DELETING FILES WITH DEL

When you no longer need a file, it's a good idea to remove it from your disk. Doing so frees up the space occupied by the file, allowing you to put something else in its place. This is part of normal disk maintenance. Some computer owners are pack rats; they keep everything. But, eventually, even 100MB hard drives fill up with stuff. So DOS users must go back and delete files they no longer need.

Deleting files is a required part of using a computer, but it's also fatal. When you delete a file—it's gone! DOS *zaps* the file from the disk, and you no longer see it listed in the directory. DOS or your applications can no longer access the file. So you want to be careful not to accidentally delete something you need.

There are two DOS commands that delete files: DEL and ERASE. Most people use DEL, but both commands will do the same thing.

Carefully type in the following:

`DEL SNACKS`

Watch your spelling and spaces. Press Enter.

Silent and swift, DEL erased the file from disk. Pull a directory to confirm that it's gone. Type in:

`DIR`

Press Enter. The file "SNACKS" is no longer on drive A. (It's gone to "bit heaven.")

Remember that the ERASE command does the same thing, but most people use DEL. (ERASE is actually a holdover from an older disk operating system, one that pre-dates DOS.)

Drive C Cleanup

For demonstration purposes, you copied two files from drive A to drive C. You also renamed one of them. Pull a directory of drive C to find the two files. Type in:

`DIR C:`

And press Enter.

On my screen I see the two files "FOOD" and "GOODIES" on drive C. These files don't need to be on drive C, so you should delete them now using the DEL command.

First, destroy the "FOOD" file by carefully typing in the following:

`DEL C:FOOD`

Note the "C:" in there. That tells DOS to delete the file "FOOD" on drive C. Press Enter. The file "FOOD" is now gone from drive C.

More File Management

Now delete the "GOODIES" file. But do this one differently. First, log to drive C. Type in the following:

```
C:
```

Press Enter. The DOS prompt should change to show a "C" instead of an "A." You're now logged to drive C. Now delete "GOODIES" by carefully typing in the following:

```
DEL GOODIES
```

There's no need to type "C:" here because you're currently logged to drive C. Press Enter.

Pull a directory to confirm that both files are gone. Type in the following:

```
DIR
```

Press Enter.

Since you were already logged to drive C, you didn't need to type a "C:" in front of "GOODIES" above. DOS assumed you meant drive C, and deleted the file "GOODIES" it found there.

Now log back to drive A by typing in the following:

```
A:
```

Press Enter.

That's the DEL command in action. You just removed two unneeded files from drive C. The original files are all still on drive A. In effect, you've just done some "housekeeping."

Just to make sure everything is okay, pull a directory of drive A. Type in:

```
DIR
```

Press Enter. Here's what I see on my screen:

```
Volume in drive A is DIRTY
Directory of A:\
ABOUT    ME       57 11-08-92 10:49a
FOOD              79 11-08-92 11:02a
HINTS            395 11-08-92 11:11a
```

```
GOODIES        79 11-08-92 11:02a
SNACKS         79 11-08-92 11:02a
    5 File(s)   357376 bytes free
```

You may have more files or files with different names if you've experimented with REN or COPY. But make sure you have at least "ABOUT.ME" "FOOD" and "HINTS"—the original three files.

POINT-OF-VIEW

There is a certain perspective DOS has on files and disk drives. When you're currently logged to drive A, you don't need to specify "A:" to refer to files on that disk. DOS just assumes you mean files on A: since you're logged there. But you must specify "C:" or "B:" to refer to files on drive C or B.

For the past few chapters, you've been copying, renaming, and deleting files between drives A and C. Since you were logged to drive A the entire time, "A:" was never specified. You could have put it down, but it would have been redundant.

Specifying a drive letter is only needed when a file exists on another drive, otherwise it's optional. Take a look at the following COPY commands. Assume you're logged to drive A:

```
COPY C:HELLO A:HELLO
COPY C:HELLO A:
COPY C:HELLO
```

They all do the same thing: copy the file "HELLO" from drive C to the current drive A. There are only varying degrees of being specific between them. As long as you're logged to drive A, you can choose any one. But suppose you're logged to drive B? Then only the following two will work:

```
COPY C:HELLO A:HELLO
COPY C:HELLO A:
```

More File Management

If you're logged to drive C, then you must be specific with the destination only. Either of the following will work if you're logged to drive C:

```
COPY C:HELLO A:HELLO
COPY HELLO A:
```

Why is this important? Because DOS accepts a variety of commands, and allows you a number of shortcuts, depending on your currently logged drive—your "point of view." Remember that DOS makes assumptions: It knows the currently logged drive. So oftentimes you don't need to specify it.

SUMMARY

Two additional, important file manipulation commands are REN/RENAME and DEL/ERASE.

The REN, or RENAME, command is used to change a file's name. You first specify a file's present name, then follow it with the new name. The new name must follow the 8-dot-3 naming pattern and contain only valid characters.

The DEL command is used to delete files. You follow DEL with the filename to delete, press Enter, and *poof!* it's gone. The ERASE command will do the same thing.

You can now remove the diskette from drive A. If you need a break, go ahead and take one. The next chapter starts off fresh with a new topic.

As a reminder, here are the steps to shutting down your PC:

1. Make sure you're at the DOS prompt.
2. Remove any floppy diskettes from the floppy drives (make sure the drive light is off).
3. Turn off all peripherals.
4. Finally, turn off the PC.

Lesson Three

The Subdirectory Tree

CHAPTER 14

Subdirectories

Disks are used to store files, and files hold information. Each disk is limited, however, in the number of files it can hold. After all, the typical floppy diskette only has some 360K of storage. If you have 36 10K files, the disk is full. But consider 100 3K files, or 200 1.5K files. Sure, the diskette could hold that many. But it would be an organizational nightmare.

DOS is about file organization, and so is the subject of this chapter. There are many reasons for organizing files on a disk, with an important one being to avoid file clutter. And it also helps to keep your work neat and organized. Organization is important, but it's a subject often overlooked until it's too late. For you, at this stage in the game, it's a perfect time to discuss file organization.

ORGANIZING MEGABYTES OF SPACE

Imagine looking at a directory listing of some 1,000 files. Your PC's screen shows only 25 lines of text at a time (and 80 columns of characters across). If you listed a directory of 1,000 files you would possibly have to look at some 40 screens of files before finding the one you want. What a terrible mess!

The typical 40 megabyte hard drive often has hundreds of files on it, and room for hundreds more. Trying to find a single file would be like looking up a friend's name in an unalphabetized phone book. Even worse, after a while you'd run out of names for files. The 8-dot-3 naming scheme doesn't promote clever names. (For example, I have about ten files on my system named CHAPT01 for "Chapter One" of a book.)

The solution is to divide a disk up into separate file areas, or *subdirectories*. Each subdirectory will hold its own files. So while there are thousands of files on disk, they're all stored in individual work areas, independent of each other.

Organizing Files

The idea of a subdirectory wasn't introduced to DOS users until IBM stuck a hard drive into their PC/XT computer in 1983. Before then, we all worked with floppy disks only.

Organization wasn't a problem with floppy disks. On one disk, you had your word processing software. Another disk had your spreadsheet. When you wanted to switch programs, you simply swapped disks.

Data files were also kept on separate diskettes. When I started writing, I kept each of my books on a separate diskette. My short stories were on their own diskette, as well. File organization was as easy as sticking the proper diskette into the drive.

Then along came the hard drive. Essentially, a hard drive is one great floppy disk. It's faster than a floppy, and can hold more information. But new hard drive users had to stop thinking of the hard drive as one great disk. So the concept of subdirectories on the PC was born.

Basically, there are two limitations to having a large disk:

1. File organization
2. Directory size

File organization is what doesn't happen when you have several hundred files on a disk. Floppy disk users originally organized their work by keeping separate files on separate diskettes. When they got a hard disk, floppy users simply copied

Subdirectories

everything over to the hard disk, putting it all on one disk. While this appeared to work all right at first, new hard disk users soon experienced organizational problems, naming conflicts, and a directory listing with hundreds of files in it.

The second limitation on a hard disk is the directory size. When you type the DIR command you see a list of files on disk. Each entry in the list represents one file. DOS only has room for so many entries in a disk's directory. The standard 360K floppy disk only has room for 112 entries in its directory. This means there can only be 112 files on a 360K floppy. No matter how big the files are, once you have 112 of them, you'll see a "diskette full" error message.

- *While there is ample space to add new files, DOS has no more directory entries, or "slots," in which to put them.*

This baffles some users to no end: "I get a 'disk full' error message and my directory listing says I have 117,000 bytes free!"

The reason for the "disk full" message is that the diskette has 112 files on it—the maximum DOS can handle. A hard drive also has a directory entry limit, but it's usually around 512 or so. Even then, no matter how big the files are, once you hit that magic number, DOS will tell you the disk is full—even with megabytes of free space left over.

So there are two problems in dealing with a large file storage device (a hard drive) with lots of files: File organization, and the limit DOS places on the number of files in a directory. All hope isn't lost, however.

The solution is subdirectories. By creating a subdirectory you're making another work area on disk for files. You can organize your files by placing all related files into that subdirectory. And DOS places no limit on the number of files you can have in a subdirectory. So subdirectories are your key to putting lots of files on a hard drive—and keeping them organized.

MAKING SUBDIRECTORIES

All disks can have subdirectories. Though they're primarily used on hard drives, you can also put them on floppy diskettes. For the following examples, you'll be using a floppy diskette. This is just for practice. Later you'll want to apply these techniques to your hard drive "for real."

Start your computer if you turned it off from the last lesson. As a review, here are the steps required to turn on your PC:

1. Turn on all necessary peripherals.
2. Turn on the computer.
3. Enter the date and time.
4. Start working with DOS.

■ *Remember to keep diskettes out of the floppy drives until you're told to insert them.*

Locate the diskette you previously labeled "Test Disk." You'll be creating a whole slew of subdirectories on it as an example. Put the diskette into your A drive and close the drive door. Then log to drive A by typing:

```
A:
```

Press Enter.

The "Root" Directory

DOS's system of subdirectories is often referred to as a *tree structure*. All disks have one main directory, called the *root*.

■ *The root directory is the main directory on a disk.*

On drive A, enter the DIR command. Type:

```
DIR
```

After pressing Enter you'll see a list of files on the disk. Those files are actually in the root directory, the main and, presently, only directory on that diskette.

Subdirectories

Take a good look at the directory listing. Below the first line (that starts with "Volume in . . .") locate the line that says:

```
Directory of A:\
```

That line tells you which *directory* you're looking at. It actually reads, "This is a list of files in the *root directory* on drive A."

From an earlier chapter, you learned that "A:" is the DOS symbol for drive A. Following that "A:" in the directory listing is a backslash character (\ ). That single backslash is DOS's symbol for the root directory. That's how you can read "Directory of A:\" as the "list of files in the root directory of drive A."

- *The symbol for the root directory is a single backslash (\ ). The other slash, the forward slash (/), is used elsewhere in DOS.*

The root directory symbol is used as a reference. DOS and all your applications can take advantage of it. Type in the following:

```
DIR \
```

That's the DIR command followed by a space and a single backslash. Can you guess what it means? Press Enter.

Again, the same directory is displayed—the root directory on drive A. With "DIR \" you told DOS to "display the root directory." Since a drive letter wasn't specified, DOS assumed you meant the current drive.

Many Roots

Each drive in your system has a root directory. Carefully type in the following:

```
DIR C:\
```

This reads, "list the files in the root directory of drive C." Press Enter. You'll see the files in the root directory of drive C listed.

Here you're using two points of view: first comes "C:," the disk drive; second comes the directory, the root (\ ) above. Both symbols are listed together to identify a specific directory on drive

C. Later you'll see how to list the contents of other subdirectories, though it's pretty much the same process.

Making a Subdirectory With MD

All disks have a root directory. Branching off from that root are *subdirectories*. Let's make a few.

The DOS command to make a directory is MKDIR, which stands for MaKe DIRectory. A shorthand version, more commonly used, is MD. To make the new subdirectory, you specify the directory's name after the MD command.

For example, to make a subdirectory called STUFF on your test diskette, type in the following:

```
MD STUFF
```

Check your typing. That's "MD" for Make Directory, followed by a space and the name of the directory DOS will create. Press Enter.

DOS has just created a directory named STUFF. It's a subdirectory off of the root directory, and you can see it in the DIR listing. Type:

```
DIR
```

Press Enter.

My diskette has the following directory listing:

```
Volume in drive A is DIRTY
Directory of A:\
ABOUT    ME       57 11-08-92 10:49a
FOOD             79 11-08-92 11:02a
HINTS           395 11-08-92 11:11a
GOODIES          79 11-08-92 11:02a
STUFF    <DIR>      11-09-92 12:01p
    5 File(s)   357376 bytes free
```

Since the subdirectory STUFF is part of the root directory, it's shown in the directory listing. STUFF appears just like any other file, but you see the characters "<DIR>" instead of a file size.

Subdirectories

Locate the "<DIR>" on your screen. That's what tells you STUFF is a subdirectory.

The "STUFF" subdirectory is now a separate work area on disk. STUFF can hold files—even other subdirectories. You'll be COPYing files to the STUFF directory in just a moment.

Making Other Subdirectories

To conclude this chapter, make two more subdirectories on the diskette in drive A. Call the first one TEMP. Type:

MD TEMP

Press Enter.

Now make a second subdirectory. Name this one BUDGET:

MD BUDGET

Press Enter.

Pull a Directory to make sure everything's in order. Type:

DIR

Press Enter. You should see something along the lines of the following:

```
Volume in drive A is DIRTY
Directory of A:\
ABOUT    ME       57 11-08-92  10:49a
FOOD              79 11-08-92  11:02a
HINTS            395 11-08-92  11:11a
GOODIES           79 11-08-92  11:02a
STUFF    <DIR>      11-09-92  12:01p
TEMP     <DIR>      11-09-92  12:05p
BUDGET   <DIR>      11-09-92  12:06p
   7 File(s)    355328 bytes free
```

The root directory on drive A now has three subdirectories: STUFF, TEMP and BUDGET.

There's one more important bit of information before concluding this introduction to subdirectories:

- *Subdirectories are named like files.*

When you create a subdirectory, you're really making a special type of file on disk. After all, the subdirectory name is listed in the DIR listing. Because of that, subdirectories are named the same as files: the standard 8-dot-3 convention, plus letters, numbers and special symbols. (Refer to Appendix B for what's kosher and what isn't in a filename.)

Very few DOS users name a subdirectory using an extension. Normally they're just one- to eight-letter names, usually describing what's in the subdirectory. For example, you'll want to put your word processing files into a WP subdirectory; DOS usually goes into a DOS subdirectory; you'd put your Great American Novel into a GRAMNO or NOVEL subdirectory, and so on.

SUMMARY

To keep your disks organized, DOS uses separate work areas on disk called *subdirectories*. Each subdirectory holds files in a unique area, separate from the other files on disk.

All disks have one main directory, the "root" directory. The root directory's symbol is the single backslash (\ ).

The root directory can only hold so many files. To add more files to the disk, and to keep them organized, you create subdirectories. This is done using the MKDIR or MD command (most people use MD because it's quicker to type).

To make a directory, you use the MD command followed by the name of the directory you want to make. Directories are named just like files, though few DOS users put an extension on the directory name.

Keep the Test Disk in your A drive for the next chapter. There you'll learn how to access the different subdirectories, as well as copy files between them.

CHAPTER 15

Working With Subdirectories

Subdirectories are the key to organizing your files, as well as the key to putting lots of files on a large hard drive. In the previous chapter you discovered the MD command, which is used to make subdirectories. This chapter continues the lesson with the commands to "log to" subdirectories, information on copying files between subdirectories, and general subdirectory maintenance.

CHANGING DIRECTORIES

To change from one drive to another, you type the drive's letter at the DOS prompt, followed by a colon, and press Enter. This is referred to as *logging* from one drive to another. The "currently logged" drive is the one you're currently using, as you can see by looking at the DOS prompt.

Subdirectories are "logged to" in the same manner. But to move from one subdirectory to another you use DOS's Change Directory command, CD or CHDIR. (As with MKDIR and MD, most DOS users use only the abbreviation, CD.)

CD is one of DOS's "dual-mode" commands. It does two things, depending on how it's used. By itself, the CD command is used to display the current directory. If you follow CD with a drive letter, it will display the current directory for that drive. But when you follow CD with the name of a subdirectory, then you'll be logged to that subdirectory. You'll change subdirectories, in effect.

Displaying the Current Directory

Let's handle CD's split personality a step at a time. At the DOS prompt, type:

CD

Press Enter.

A:\

You've just asked DOS to display the Current Directory (CD), and "A:\" was its response. The "A:" means that you're currently logged to drive A. After the colon, you see the name of the current directory. The single backslash is used to represent the root directory. You're currently logged to the root directory on drive A.

- *CD by itself basically "tells you where you are" on your disk drive system. It displays the currently logged disk drive and subdirectory.*

When you follow CD with a disk drive letter, it will tell you the current directory for that drive. Type the following:

CD C:

Press Enter and you'll see:

C:\

On drive C, the root directory is also the current directory.

Normally, using CD with its "drive" option is rare. Most of the time, CD is used to change to another subdirectory on the same drive.

Changing to Another Directory

CD is your primary hard disk navigational tool. When followed by the name of a subdirectory, CD will Change Directories,

Working With Subdirectories

making the named subdirectory the current directory. Type the following:

CD STUFF

This tells DOS to change to the directory STUFF. (Remember that STUFF is a subdirectory on drive A.) Press Enter.

Not much may have happened. But you're presently logged to the STUFF subdirectory on drive A. To prove it, type CD alone to display the current directory. Type:

CD

Press Enter. You'll see:

A:\STUFF

Here's another clue. Type the following:

DIR

Press Enter. You'll see something like this:

```
Volume in drive A has no label
Directory of A:\STUFF
.            <DIR>    10-30-92   2:17p
..           <DIR>    10-30-92   2:17p
    2 File(s)     356352 bytes free
```

Since you didn't give it any parameters, DIR displayed a list of files in the current directory. There are still files in the root directory, but this directory listing doesn't show them.

Remember that each subdirectory is a different work area on disk, containing its own files. If you don't specify any parameters, the DIR command assumes you mean the current disk drive *and* the currently logged subdirectory.

Locate the second line in your directory listing. It says "Directory of A:\STUFF." That tells you that you're seeing a list of files in the directory STUFF, which is a subdirectory of the root directory (\), which is on drive A.

You'll also notice that STUFF seems to have magically acquired two files. Both have "forbidden" names: dot and dot-dot. Yet, both are directory entries. These oddities are covered toward the end of the chapter.

Changing Back to the Root

To change back to the root directory, you specify its symbol after the CD command. Type in the following:

CD \

Press Enter and you'll be back at the root. Type the following:

DIR

Press Enter.

Since you're now "logged to" the root directory, the DIR command displays only the files there.

Working With Several Levels

Log to the BUDGET subdirectory. Type:

CD BUDGET

Press Enter. You're now in the BUDGET subdirectory. Confirm this by typing in the following:

CD

Press Enter.

A:\BUDGET

So far all the subdirectories on your diskette exist off the root directory. DOS still holds a limit on the maximum number of files you can have in the root. But it doesn't limit the number of files in a subdirectory. And one type of file you can have in a subdirectory is another subdirectory.

Type in the following:

MD JAN

Press Enter.

Working With Subdirectories

You've just created a subdirectory JAN in the subdirectory BUDGET—a sub-subdirectory (though they're all called "subdirectories").

Type in the DIR command to see how JAN looks inside the BUDGET subdirectory:

```
DIR
```

After pressing Enter, you'll see something like the following:

```
Volume in drive A has no label
Directory of A:\BUDGET
.         <DIR>    10-30-92   2:23p
..        <DIR>    10-30-92   2:23p
JAN       <DIR>    10-30-92   2:45p
    3 File(s)    355328 bytes free
```

There's JAN, a real subdirectory inside the BUDGET subdirectory (which is all under the root directory). Let's CD to JAN. Type in the following:

```
CD JAN
```

Press Enter. Now enter the CD command to have DOS tell you just exactly where you are. Type:

```
CD
```

Press Enter. You'll see:

```
A:\BUDGET\JAN
```

There is really no limit on the number of subdirectories you can have on a disk. For practical purposes, however, you should stack subdirectories only a few layers deep. Most people rarely go below four levels.

Remember the theme here: *organization*. The budget subdirectory may wind up having 12 subdirectories of its own, one for each month of the year (JAN through DEC). Into each subdirectory you'll place files dealing with that month's budget. That's organization.

PATHNAMES

As long as you're getting several layers deep into subdirectories, you should be formally introduced to the concept of the *pathname*. As the name implies, a pathname is both a direction and a location. It's the name of a specific subdirectory on disk.

When you type the CD command by itself, it displays a pathname.

```
A:\BUDGET\JAN
```

This is the full pathname of the subdirectory JAN. The pathname tells you that JAN is a subdirectory of BUDGET, which is a subdirectory of the root directory on drive A.

A: —Drive A

A:\ —The root directory on drive A

A:\BUDGET —The BUDGET subdirectory under the root directory

A:\BUDGET\JAN —JAN under BUDGET under the root directory

You'll note that in a pathname, the backslash character is used as a separator between subdirectories.

- *The backslash character separates subdirectories in a path.*

Everything starts with the single backslash, the root. Below that, subdirectories are each separated by backslashes.

Pathnames can get quite lengthy, but as long as you only go down three or four subdirectory levels, they'll never get too complex. DOS does, however, place a limit on the size of a pathname: A complete pathname can be no more than 63 characters long—including the drive letter, colon and all the backslash separators. That's about the only limit DOS places on how "deep" you can go with subdirectories.

Working With Subdirectories

Parents and Children

Other pathname and subdirectory terminology includes the terms "parent directory" and "child directory." This almost makes the subdirectory tree look more like a family tree!

In A:\BUDGET\JAN, the root directory is the *parent* of BUDGET. JAN is BUDGET's *child*. The root directory has no parent (it can't). And presently JAN has no child directories.

This familial stuff is reference material. Oftentimes you'll hear jargon such as "log to the parent directory." That just means log to the directory immediately "above" the current directory, the next directory to the left in the pathname.

CDing Around

The CD command is your main subdirectory navigational tool. And it's quite powerful. But CD isn't just followed by the name of a subdirectory. It's followed by a *pathname*.

Presently, you're logged to the A:\BUDGET\JAN subdirectory on drive A. To log to the TEMP subdirectory you simply specify TEMP's pathname after CD.

Carefully type in the following:

```
CD \TEMP
```

Press Enter. You're now in the TEMP subdirectory. To prove it, type:

```
CD
```

Press Enter.

```
A:\TEMP
```

Let's now move back to the A:\BUDGET\JAN subdirectory. Carefully type in the following:

```
CD \BUDGET\JAN
```

Here, the full pathname is again specified. Press Enter and you'll once again be logged to A:\BUDGET\JAN. (Type CD to prove it.)

Now move to the root directory. Type:

CD \

Press Enter. The single backslash moves you up to the root directory.

- *You can move to any subdirectory on your disk simply by specifying its full pathname after CD.*

THE TREE

Going back to the start of the previous chapter, remember how this directory system is referred to as a "tree structure"? Consider Figure 15.2.

The "root" is at the top of this upside-down tree. Underneath it are three file storage areas: the subdirectories STUFF, TEMP and BUDGET. BUDGET has a single child directory, JAN. If you were to visualize subdirectory storage—the tree—this is one way it might appear.

Dot and Dot-Dot

Change directories to the STUFF subdirectory. Type in the following:

CD \STUFF

Press Enter. Now pull a directory. Type:

DIR

Press Enter.

Find the two dot entries in the directory listing. All subdirectories have those curious little entries. They aren't files. Instead, they're abbreviations.

The dot and dot-dot directory entries are created by DOS and you'll see them in all subdirectories. The double dot entry is an abbreviation for the parent directory. It's DOS's link between the current directory and its parent. The single dot entry represents the subdirectory itself.

Working With Subdirectories

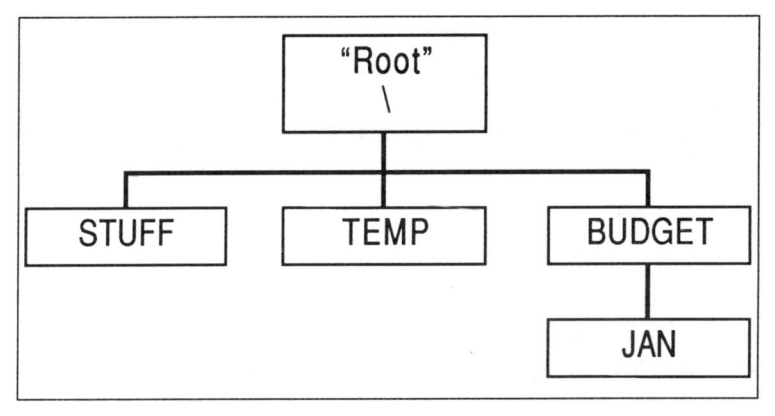

```
                    ┌─────────┐
                    │ "Root"  │
                    │    \    │
                    └────┬────┘
          ┌──────────────┼──────────────┐
     ┌────┴───┐     ┌────┴───┐     ┌────┴───┐
     │ STUFF  │     │  TEMP  │     │ BUDGET │
     └────────┘     └────────┘     └────┬───┘
                                        │
                                   ┌────┴───┐
                                   │  JAN   │
                                   └────────┘
```

Figure 15.2: The tree structure.

- *The double dot entry is an abbreviation for the parent directory. The single dot abbreviation represents the current directory.*

These abbreviations can be used in pathnames, and often come in handy with the CD command. For example, type in the following:

CD ..

This command expands out to read, "change to the parent directory." You don't need to spell out the parent directory's full path that way (and it's easier to type). Press Enter.

You're now at the root directory—which is STUFF's parent directory. To prove it, type in:

CD

Press Enter.

A:\

Dot-dot is both an abbreviation and a shortcut. It really comes in handy when you're several layers deep in the subdirectory tree, saving you time from typing a long path just to get to the parent directory.

Note that the root directory doesn't have a dot-dot directory entry (no parent). It does, however, have a dot entry, which represents itself (the root directory). But the single dot for the root directory isn't displayed by the DIR command.

SUMMARY

The CD or CHDIR command is central to using subdirectories. By itself, CD displays the currently logged subdirectory (actually a pathname). When used with a drive letter, CD displays the currently logged directory on that drive.

CD's real strength is in its Change Directory mode. When you follow CD with the name of a directory, that directory becomes the current directory. Or, to put it another way, you use CD to "log" to another subdirectory on the same disk.

The term "pathname" is used to describe a subdirectory's location. The pathname starts with the disk drive letter and colon. Following that is the subdirectory's parentage, starting with the root directory (a single backslash), and all parent directories, each separated by a single backslash.

Finally, the dot and dot-dot entries in a directory listing are used to represent the parent and current directory. They come in handy for use with the CD command to change to the parent directory.

The following chapter concludes this important exploration of subdirectories with file manipulation between subdirectories, and directory management. Keep your PC on and the diskette in drive A.

CHAPTER 16

File Management and Subdirectories

The subject of subdirectories is really the domain of "hard disk management." Quite a few beginner's books on DOS skirt around the subject. Yet subdirectories are such a central part to using DOS, DOS applications, and file management, that it has to be part of the bare DOS essentials.

This chapter concludes the subdirectory trilogy. You know how to make directories and how to change between them. The subject now is copying files between subdirectories using the COPY command. Also covered here is the third of DOS's three subdirectory commands, RMDIR or RD, which is used to delete or remove subdirectories.

COPYING FILES BETWEEN SUBDIRECTORIES

In Chapter 12, you learned about the "source" and "destination" parts of the COPY command:

```
COPY source destination
```

Source and destination are filenames, the source being the original and destination being the location of the duplicate, or the name of the duplicate if a copy was made on the same drive. (Refer back to Chapter 12 if you need to bone up.)

But source and destination can be more than just filenames and disk drive letters. They can, in fact, be full pathnames.

Using Pathnames

When you used COPY earlier, you duplicated files on one drive or copied files from one drive to another. But what COPY was really doing was copying files from one pathname to another pathname. (Now that you've been introduced to the concept of subdirectories, you can finally know the truth.)

DOS does a lot of assuming. When you copied a file from drive A to drive C in Chapter 12, you were really copying a file from the root directory of drive A to the root directory of drive C:

```
COPY FOOD C:
```

Since both disks were logged to the root directory, you didn't need to specify the backslash. Yet DOS assumed the backslash because you didn't tell it otherwise. Each of the following commands could have been substituted for the above:

```
COPY FOOD C:
COPY \FOOD C:
COPY A:\FOOD C:
COPY A:\FOOD C:\
```

Again, this all branches back to point of view and how specific you need to get with DOS. (For example, you don't have to name the destination filename "FOOD"; DOS will do that unless you specify otherwise.)

COPYing From One Subdirectory to Another

Right now you're logged to the root directory of drive A. Type the following:

```
DIR
```

Press Enter.

You should see a list of files, plus three subdirectories.

Copy the file "FOOD" to the TEMP subdirectory. "FOOD" is the source, and the TEMP subdirectory is the destination. Carefully type in the following:

```
COPY A:\FOOD A:\TEMP
```

File Management and Subdirectories 135

The source is "A:\FOOD," the file "FOOD" in the root directory of drive A. The destination is "A:\TEMP," the subdirectory TEMP in drive A. Double check your typing and press Enter.

```
1 File(s) copied
```

A copy of the file "FOOD" now exists in the TEMP subdirectory. The duplicate file has the same name as the original. To confirm this, pull a directory of the TEMP subdirectory. Type in the following:

```
DIR A:\TEMP
```

Make sure you've typed correctly, then press Enter. Look for the file "FOOD" in the directory listing of the TEMP subdirectory.

Some Shortcuts

The last two commands you typed were very specific. To copy a file to a subdirectory on the same drive, you typed the following:

```
COPY A:\FOOD A:\TEMP
```

But you're already on drive A, so you could have just typed:

```
COPY \FOOD \TEMP
```

And you're already in the root directory, so you could have knocked the initial backslash off as well:

```
COPY FOOD TEMP
```

This may confuse you. It's hard to tell that TEMP is a subdirectory and not another file. But DOS knows. Type in the following:

```
COPY GOODIES TEMP
```

Press Enter.

```
1 File(s) copied
```

The file "GOODIES" will be copied to the subdirectory TEMP. You didn't need to specify "A:" nor the root directory symbol. DOS knows which drive you're logged to and that you're already in the root directory.

These same assumptions are made for the DIR command as well. Above, you typed the following to pull a directory for the TEMP subdirectory:

```
DIR A:\TEMP
```

The following would have worked as well:

```
DIR \TEMP
```

As would have this:

```
DIR TEMP
```

DOS knows the drive is "A:" and that you're in the root directory. So why be redundant? Type in the following:

```
DIR TEMP
```

Press Enter. You'll see something like the following:

```
Volume in drive A is DIRTY
Directory of A:\TEMP
.            <DIR>     11-09-92  11:05a
..           <DIR>     11-09-92  11:05a
FOOD            79     11-08-92  11:02a
GOODIES         79     11-08-92  11:02a
    4 File(s)    352256 bytes free
```

There are your two files, each safely copied into the TEMP subdirectory.

COPYing With a Different Name

In Chapter 12, you saw how COPY created a file duplicate and gave it a new name. Though you may not remember it, you once typed in the following command:

```
COPY FOOD C:SNACKS
```

The file "FOOD" was copied to drive C and given "SNACKS" as a new name. You can do the same thing between subdirectories, giving the destination copy of the file a new name. To do so, you must understand one additional element of a pathname: the final backslash separator.

File Management and Subdirectories

A pathname gives the exact location of a subdirectory or file. If the pathname indicates a file, then the filename must be separated from its subdirectory name by a backslash. For example:

`A:\TEMP\FOOD`

The above is the full pathname for the FOOD file you just copied to the TEMP subdirectory. It breaks down as follows:

A:—The disk drive

\TEMP\—The subdirectories

FOOD—The filename

"\TEMP\" means the directory TEMP under the root directory. That trailing backslash is the one that separates the subdirectories from the filename.

COPY the file "FOOD" to the TEMP subdirectory again. This time, give it "EATS" as a new name. Carefully type the following:

`COPY FOOD A:\TEMP\EATS`

Press Enter.

`1 File(s) copied`

"A:\TEMP\EATS" is a full pathname. "A:" is the drive letter, "\TEMP\" is the subdirectory, and "EATS" is the new filename. Of course, the first part, "A:\" is redundant. The following command would have produced the same results:

`COPY FOOD TEMP\EATS`

This is just a little bit more confusing, and very non-specific. But it works the same.

Checking Your Work

You now have three files in the TEMP subdirectory on drive A. To check for their existence, you use the DIR command. The DIR command is how you see which files you have on disk. True, you could write them down on a piece of paper. But why, when the DIR command is so handy to type?

Type the following:

File Management and Subdirectories

```
DIR TEMP
```

This tells DOS to pull a directory of the subdirectory TEMP on drive A. (You could have specified "A:\TEMP"—but that's redundant.) Press Enter.

You should see something like the following:

```
Volume in drive A is DIRTY
Directory of A:\TEMP
.            <DIR>     11-09-92  11:05a
..           <DIR>     11-09-92  11:05a
FOOD            79     11-08-92  11:02a
GOODIES         79     11-08-92  11:02a
EATS            79     11-08-92  11:02a
    5 File(s)    351232 bytes free
```

How about this for curiosities: The diskette in drive A now has two files with exactly the same name. There are two "FOOD" files. Two files with the same name now exist on one diskette in drive A. Isn't that impossible?

Yes, it is impossible. But since both files are in separate work areas, DOS doesn't care.

■ *Your disk can have dozens of files with the same name. As long as they're in different subdirectories, it's okay.*

Type the following to log to the TEMP subdirectory:

```
CD \TEMP
```

Press Enter. Now issue the DIR command again. Type:

```
DIR
```

Press Enter.

The DIR command only displays files in the current directory. Each subdirectory is independent of other subdirectories on a disk. While you're in one subdirectory, DOS ignores the files in all other subdirectories. The only way around this is if you specify a file's pathname when using a DOS command.

File Management and Subdirectories   *139*

For example, the "HINTS" file is on the diskette in drive A. Type in the following:

```
TYPE HINTS
```

Remember that the TYPE command lists the contents of a file. Press Enter.

```
File not found
```

Though "HINTS" is on drive A, it's not in the current directory. DOS cannot "see" outside of the current directory, so you get an error. Now type in this DOS command:

```
TYPE \HINTS
```

Here you're telling DOS something more specific: "Look for the file 'HINTS' in the root directory." Press Enter.

- *Always use a full pathname if the file isn't in the current directory. Or, you can log to that other directory using CD, and then access the file.*

You must always be in a directory to access its files, or at least specify a full path to that file. The same holds true for files with the same names. But remember that though two files will share the same name, they're not the same file. For example, on my hard drive I have seven "CHAPT01" files. Though they all have the same name, they're in different subdirectories. And the contents of each are different.

DIRECTORY MAINTENANCE

There is an organizational aspect of files and directories that just can't be shown here. When you start using your computer system "for real," you'll be putting applications in their own subdirectories. The data files for those directories will probably be in their own subdirectories, under the application subdirectories. (I'm getting good at typing the word "subdirectories.")

One facet of using subdirectories not yet covered is getting rid of them. Occasionally you'll want to do this, but it's not something done often.

Removing Subdirectories

Subdirectories are removed with the RMDIR or RD command, which stands for ReMove DIRectory. As with MKDIR and CHDIR, most DOS users prefer to type RD over RMDIR.

RD works like the DEL command, which removes files. You simply specify the name of the subdirectory to delete and RD removes it. But there are a few rules to follow before you can do this.

RULE #1: Before you can delete a subdirectory it must be "empty." All files and any sub-subdirectories must be removed from a directory before you can RD it.

RULE #2: You cannot delete a subdirectory if you're currently logged to it. Most people first delete all files from a subdirectory, then log to the parent directory before RDing.

Change back to the root directory of drive A. Type:

```
CD \
```

Press Enter.

The subdirectory STUFF is empty. Confirm that by typing:

```
DIR STUFF
```

Press Enter.

You should only see the two dot entries listed in STUFF, meaning the directory is essentially empty. To remove it type in the following:

```
RD \STUFF
```

Press Enter. STUFF is gone!

Now remove the subdirectory TEMP. But remember that TEMP contains three files. Before you remove TEMP you'll have to delete those files. Type in the following:

```
DEL \TEMP\FOOD
```

Press Enter. The file "FOOD" in the TEMP subdirectory is gone. But that pathname is a long thing to type, and it's easy to make mistakes. Instead of doing that two more times, change to the TEMP subdirectory. Type in the following:

File Management and Subdirectories

```
CD \TEMP
```

Press Enter. Now you can delete the two remaining files. First type in:

```
DEL GOODIES
```

Press Enter. (The full pathname isn't required because you're now logged to the TEMP subdirectory.) To delete the final file, type in:

```
DEL EATS
```

Press Enter.

Now delete the TEMP subdirectory by typing:

```
RD TEMP
```

Press Enter.

```
Invalid path, not directory,
or directory not empty
```

Oops! You're still logged to the TEMP subdirectory. And rule number two states that you can't delete a subdirectory if you're currently logged to it. Log to the root directory by typing in:

```
CD \
```

Press Enter. Now you can delete the TEMP subdirectory. Type in the following:

```
RD TEMP
```

Press Enter and it's gone.

Things You Can't Do With Subdirectories

Subdirectory maintenance isn't something you'll do often. Removing subdirectories simply means you didn't think far enough ahead when you originally designed your disk's organization. But two other things you may want to do with subdirectories are move them and rename them. Unfortunately, DOS won't let you do either.

■ *You cannot rename a subdirectory once it's created.*

DOS has no REN or RENAME command for a subdirectory. True, a subdirectory is a file and it seems like REN would rename it just as it renames files. But it won't work. If you try it, you'll get an error.

- *You cannot move a subdirectory or "tree branch" once it's created.*

DOS also has no MOVE command, and COPY will not let you copy a subdirectory structure from one place to another.

There are special programs called *utilities* that will allow you to rename directories. And special applications called *DOS shells* will let you move subdirectories around. In keeping with the tree metaphor, moving and copying directories is referred to as "prune and graft." Though DOS won't let you do it, there are other programs available that will.

SUMMARY

The COPY command can be used to copy files from one subdirectory to another. You simply specify the full pathname for the file's source and destination. For example:

```
COPY A:\FOOD A:\TEMP\EATS
```

Of course, if you're already logged to the root directory of drive A, the "A:\," the source and destination are optional.

In a full pathname, such as "A:\TEMP\EATS," note that a trailing backslash is added after the final subdirectory name. This is required when dealing with files in other subdirectories.

To remove a subdirectory, the RD command is used. But before you can remove a directory, it must be empty of files and you cannot be logged to the subdirectory you're deleting.

Additional information on the subdirectory commands is provided in your DOS manual. For now, keep your computer on and the disk in drive A for the next chapter.

CHAPTER 17

More DIR Command Stuff

The DIR command is one of the most useful DOS commands. Basically, it lists files on disk. Actually, now that you know about subdirectories, I can tell you that DIR lists files in the current subdirectory (or another subdirectory if it's specified).

This chapter is about the DIR command and looking at files on disk. The DIR command was introduced in Chapter 5, but only touched upon briefly. Here, the full detail of DIR is covered, along with some optional switches and tricks for printing a directory.

ANOTHER LOOK AT THE DIRECTORY

Log to drive C, your hard drive. Type:

```
C:
```

Press Enter.

Somewhere on your hard drive should be a DOS subdirectory. It's where all your DOS files and programs are stored. Usually the subdirectory is named "DOS" and it's right off the root directory. Pull a directory of your hard drive to look for DOS. Type:

```
DIR
```

Press Enter. The DOS subdirectory might be found in your root directory. Scan the directory listing for something that looks like this:

```
DOS      <DIR>   8-24-90  4:45p
```

Once you find the DOS subdirectory, log to it. For example, if you found the above listing in the root directory, you'd type:

```
CD \DOS
```

Press Enter.

Some hard drives may have DOS stored in a sub-subdirectory. Its files might be found in \SYSTEM\DOS or maybe even \BIN\DOS. For example, one of my personal computers has DOS located in the \SYSTEM\DOS subdirectory. To get to it, I type "CD \SYSTEM\DOS" and press Enter. If you can't find the DOS subdirectory on your hard drive, contact your dealer or whoever set up your computer.

Locating Files

DOS has two types of commands: internal and external. DOS keeps internal commands in the computer's memory. When you type COPY, REN, CLS, DEL, and so on, those commands are a part of the DOS program already in memory.

External commands are the names of DOS programs on disk. FORMAT is a DOS command, yet it's also the name of a program file DOS stores on disk. DOS comes with about forty-or-so such external commands. And on most PCs, they're stored in a DOS subdirectory.

You should presently be logged to the DOS subdirectory. Use the DIR command to take a look at DOS's files. Type:

```
DIR
```

Press Enter.

On my screen I saw 48 files whiz by. (I know that because it says "48 File(s)" on the bottom of the screen.) The number of files you see depends on your version of DOS and how your computer was set up.

All of those files support DOS. Some of them are the external commands, such as FORMAT. (In fact, all files with an EXE or

More DIR Command Stuff

COM filename extension are external DOS commands.) Other files fall into specific categories, but everything there is DOS.

Try to find the file "FORMAT.COM" (or it could be "FORMAT.EXE") in the listing. If you can see it on your screen, you're lucky. Otherwise, type DIR again. Look quickly!

If you can find "FORMAT.COM" then great! Otherwise, you've discovered a problem with the DIR command: The text scrolls by too quickly for you to see anything. DIR is an important command and you need to see those files. Fortunately, DOS knows this and there are ways to hunt down files in the DIR listing.

Pausing the File List

Just as the FORMAT command has optional parameters, or "switches," so does the DIR command. Type the following:

```
DIR /P
```

That's a forward slash—not a backslash. Press Enter.

You'll see the first 23 or 24 files in the DOS subdirectory displayed. At the bottom of the screen you'll see a message such as:

```
Strike a key when ready . . .
```

The "/P" typed after the DIR command is an optional parameter—a switch. When you enter "DIR /P" the directory listing will pause after each screen/page, allowing you to look over the files. You can examine the list, then press Enter when you're done to see the next screenful of files.

Press Enter now.

See how another screenful of files scrolls up the display? Keep pressing Enter after each screen until you're back to the DOS prompt.

Did you find the "FORMAT" file? If not, type in the following again and remember to look for "FORMAT":

```
DIR /P
```

Press Enter.

Another Way to Pause

Another way to pause the DIR listing, or any listing on the screen (such as when you TYPE a long text file) is by using some of the keyboard tricks you learned in Chapter 4.

Get ready to type a Control-S to pause the directory listing. Type in:

DIR

Now press Enter, and then type a Control-S. (Hold down the Ctrl key and type an S.)

Control-S pauses the display. Press any other key to start the screen scrolling again. If you want to pause a second time, press Control-S again.

> ■ *You can press Control-S once to pause a long display. A trick is to press Control-S (which qualifies as "any other key") to start the display again. But note that every other time you press Control-S, the display will pause.*

If your keyboard has a Pause or Hold key, you can also use it to pause the display. But remember to press Enter to start things up again.

A way to stop a long listing is to press Control-C or Control-Break. Doing so cancels the current DOS command and immediately returns you to the DOS prompt.

Get ready to type a Control-C. First, type in the following:

DIR

Now press Enter, then after a moment press Control-C (hold down the Ctrl key and type a C).

^C

The listing stops after you press Control-C. Look on your screen for the "^C" character. That marks the exact spot where you pressed Control-C to cancel the directory listing.

More DIR Command Stuff

The W-i-d-e Look

Type in the following:

```
DIR /W
```

Again, note the forward slash. Press Enter.

The /W switch is the *wide* switch. It displays the files in the current directory across the screen using only their filenames. If you need to locate a specific file, this is one quick way to do it. Also, the /W switch eliminates some of the technical information from the directory listing.

Can you find the "FORMAT" file now?

Finding Specific Files

For the most part, files in a directory listing are listed in a seemingly haphazard way. That's not entirely the truth. The files are listed in the order you created them or that they were copied from another drive or directory. They're not listed in alphabetical order, nor by date and time, nor by size. (If they are, then it's just a coincidence.)

If you are interested in looking for a specific file, you can use the DIR command followed by that file's name. For example, type the following:

```
DIR FORMAT.COM
```

Check your typing. Press Enter. Here's what I saw on my screen:

```
Volume in drive C is HARD DISK
Directory of C:\DOS
FORMAT   COM   11616  3-18-87 12:00p
    1 File(s)  15462400 bytes free
```

Say you don't know if FORMAT is a COM or EXE type of file. Type in the following:

```
DIR FORMAT
```

Note that FORMAT is not followed by a period. Press Enter.

If you don't specify a file extension, then DOS will show you all files that have "FORMAT" as their name. If there aren't any files starting that way, then you'll get a "file not found" error message.

- *This trick doesn't work with partial filenames. For instance, you can't type in "DIR F" to see all files starting with the letter F. There are ways to do that using DOS* filename wildcards, *which are covered in the next chapter.*

PRINTING THE DIRECTORY

Computer information printed on paper is referred to as *hard copy*. You will often work all day on your word processor and never print a character. (So far, I've written almost 70 percent of this book and not one chapter has been printed.) Eventually, you'll issue some command that will cause your work to be printed. The end result? Hard copy.

A directory listing contains an important list of files on disk. Often you'll need a hard copy of that list for reference purposes. The following sections describe various techniques for getting a hard copy of your DIR listing.

Print Screen

The Print Screen key, which may be labeled "Print Scrn," "PrtSc," or any number of combinations (but close enough so that you get the hint), is a fun key to play with. After pressing Print Screen, all the text on your screen will be sent the printer.

Before playing with Print Screen, here's a very healthy word of advice:

- *Always have your printer on and ready to print before you start to print.*

If the printer isn't on, DOS will wait for it. And wait. And wait. You may think your computer is broken or has "crashed." But it's just waiting for you to turn on the printer. (Also, make sure the

More DIR Command Stuff

printer is "selected" or "on-line." Refer to your printer's awful manual if you have trouble turning it on.)

With your printer on and loaded with paper, press the Print Screen key. (On older PCs you may have to press Shift-PrtSc.)

Zip-zip-zip. Whatever text was displayed on your screen is now on your printer. (If you have a laser printer, then the paper is still in the printer. A laser printer won't print until you've sent it a full page of information.)

To make the printer spit out the page, press its "Select" or "On-line" button, then its "Form Feed" button. That ejects a page out of the printer (and causes the laser printer to print its page). Remember to press "Select" or "On-line" a second time to put the printer back into "ready mode."

What you've just produced is called a *screen dump*, a rather unflattering term for copying all the text on your PC's screen to a page in the printer. Nearly every computer can do this. But before thinking you've discovered something magic, note that a screen dump doesn't work for graphics, nor will most printers properly print some special characters that may be on your screen. For printing a directory listing, however, it's fine.

Type the following:

```
DIR /P
```

Press Enter.

The first screenful of files will scroll up your screen. Now press the Print Screen key.

You've just produced a hard copy of the first several listings in your DOS subdirectory. Did you notice how pressing the Print Screen key didn't work like pressing Enter? Though the message on the screen says to "press any key," the Print Screen key isn't one of them. It always produces the screen dump.

Press Enter to display the next screenful of files. Then press Print Screen to print them. Keep this up until all screens have been displayed, and each one has been printed. (Press Print Screen, Enter; Print Screen, Enter; until you're back at the DOS prompt.)

When you're done, eject the final page from the printer by pressing the "On-line" or "Select" button and then pressing "Form feed." (Remember to put the printer back into ready mode by pressing "On-line" or "Select" after the page has been ejected.)

Ta-da! You have a hard copy of your directory listing. But it's just not as perfect as it could be.

Echo-to-Printer

Isn't the Print Screen key neat? But don't get too excited. Very few people use the Print Screen key. Why? It's a pain. Oftentimes you'll accidentally hit it, and usually when the printer is off. Your PC then waits for you to turn on the printer to print something you didn't want in the first place. Or worse, you press Print Screen while you're printing something else and it gets totally messed up.

While Print Screen does have its place, a better way to get a hard copy of the directory listing is with DOS's *Echo-to-printer* command. Make sure your printer is on and ready to print.

Press Control-P. (Hold down the Ctrl key and type a P.)

You've now turned on DOS's Echo-to-printer function. Everything you see on the screen will now be sent to the printer. It's what's called "dual-output" (though that's not a term worth memorizing). Type:

```
DIR
```

Press Enter.

At the same time the directory is listed on your screen, a copy is also being sent to the printer.

Turn Echo-to-printer off by typing Control-P a second time.

Control-P is what's referred to as a *toggle*. It's one key that turns something both on and off. Press Control-P once and Echo-to-printer is on. Press it again and you turn it off.

The Control-P method is about the easiest way to get information DOS displays copied to the printer. In fact, you could echo an entire DOS session to the printer just by turning on Echo-to-printer and leaving it on. Remember to toggle it off when you're done.

More DIR Command Stuff

SUMMARY

The DIR command is one of the most useful DOS commands, displaying a list of files in the current drive and directory. But you already knew that. What you learned here were the DIR command's two switches, /P and /W.

The /P switch is used to display a directory listing a screenful at a time. Between each screen, DOS displays a message and waits for you to press any key. The same effect can also be achieved by using Control-S or the Pause key on your keyboard.

The /W switch is used to display a directory in the wide format. Only the filenames are displayed in a five column format.

To print a directory listing you have a number of options. The first is to press the Print Screen button while using the DIR command's /P switch. But this "screen dump" method is rather awkward.

A better way to print is to turn on DOS's Echo-to-printer function by using the Control-P command. Control-P is also a toggle; press it once to turn it on and again to turn it off.

Keep your computer up and running for the next chapter, on wildcards.

CHAPTER 18

Wildcards

A wildcard is something that can be anything. Some big time, penny-ante, family room gamblers play poker with certain cards designated as "wild." With 10s, 6s, and 4s wild, your chances of getting a winning poker hand are greatly improved. And in the kid's game "Crazy 8s," the 8 card is wild, matching whichever card is atop the discard pile.

This chapter is about DOS's filename *wildcards*. While they won't win you that sizable 30 cent pot in poker, they do let you manipulate groups of files at a time. You can match files, copy a group of matching files, or use DOS commands to manipulate an entire disk full of files simply by using wildcards.

WORKING WITH GROUPS OF FILES

Up until now, you've been using the COPY, REN, and DEL commands with only a single file at a time. There is a way, however, to work with an entire group of files by using wildcards.

In DOS, a wildcard is placed into a filename to represent all combinations of characters at a certain position in the filename. DOS's file manipulation commands will deal with all matching filenames as a group when a wildcard-filename is specified.

There are two wildcard characters in DOS: the question mark (?), and the asterisk (*).

The ? Wildcard

The question mark wildcard is used to represent any single character in a filename.

- *The ? character represents any character in either the filename or its extension.*

Make sure you're logged to the DOS subdirectory. Type the following:

```
CD
```

Press Enter. You should see "C:\DOS" or some other directory displayed, the directory where your DOS files are located. (If not, follow the instructions in the previous chapter for logging to your DOS subdirectory on drive C.)

To test the ? wildcard, type in the following:

```
DIR MO?E
```

Press Enter.

The DIR command will list all files that start with MO and end in E. You'll probably see something like the following displayed:

```
Volume in drive C is HARD DISK
Directory of C:\DOS
MODE    COM   15487  3-17-87 12:00p
MORE    COM     313  3-17-87 12:00p
   2 File(s) 15462400 bytes free
```

Two matches were found by DOS: the "MODE.COM" and "MORE.COM" files.

Type in the following:

```
DIR ????.COM
```

Press Enter. The single question mark wildcard matches all files on disk that have *up to* four characters in their name, and COM in the filename extension. You now see them displayed on your screen. (I saw five of them.)

All file manipulation commands (DIR, COPY, REN, etc.) will

Wildcards

deal with all those matching files as a group. Let's copy all those files to drive A.

Insert your diskette labeled "Test Disk" into drive A if it's not already there. Close the drive door.

Type in the following:

```
COPY ?????.COM A:\
```

This reads, "COPY all the files with up to five characters in their names and ending in COM to the root directory of drive A." Double check your typing, and press Enter.

You'll see something like the following displayed:

```
KEYB.COM
MODE.COM
MORE.COM
SYS.COM
TREE.COM
    5 File(s) copied
```

When COPY moves a group of files, they're displayed on the screen. Now each of those files has been copied to drive A. To prove it, pull a directory of drive A. Type in the following:

```
DIR A:\
```

Press Enter. Look for the copied files to confirm they're there.

The * Wildcard

The asterisk wildcard is used to represent a group of characters in a filename.

- *The * character represents a group of characters in either the filename or its extension.*

This can be quite powerful. Type in the following:

```
DIR D*.COM
```

The DIR command will list all files that start with a D and have a COM extension. That's all files, no matter how long their name, from D.COM through DZZZZZZZ.COM. Press Enter. You'll see something like the following displayed:

```
Volume in drive C is HARD DISK
Directory of C:\DOS
DEBUG      COM    15897  3-17-87 12:00p
DISKCOMP   COM     5879  3-17-87 12:00p
DISKCOPY   COM     6295  3-17-87 12:00p
    3 File(s) 15462400 bytes free
```

Type the following:

`DIR *.COM`

Here, the wildcard represents all files that end with a COM extension. For trivial purposes, it's pronounced "star-dot-COM." To see that group of files listed, press Enter.

Here is where wildcards get their power. You can deal with a group of filenames all having the same extension simply by specifying a wildcard.

Type the following:

`COPY *.SYS A:\`

Make sure you've typed that in exactly, then look it over and guess what it does.

Press Enter.

DOS copies several files, all ending with the SYS extension, to the root directory on drive A. (The number of files copied on your system might be different.) On my screen, I saw:

```
ANSI.SYS
COUNTRY.SYS
DISPLAY.SYS
DRIVER.SYS
KEYBOARD.SYS
PRINTER.SYS
VDISK.SYS
    7 File(s) copied
```

Wildcards

Those seven files, all ending with SYS, are now on drive A. That's the power behind using wildcards.

File Management and Wildcards

Log to drive A. Type:

```
A:
```

Press Enter. Now pull a directory to look over the files you've copied so far. Type in the following:

```
DIR
```

Press Enter. You'll see a variety of files, in addition to the originals you created a while back.

You've already had a little taste of using wildcards with the DIR and COPY commands. But they can also be used with REN and DEL. Type in the following:

```
REN *.SYS *.BRO
```

Check your typing, and press Enter.

Unlike the COPY command, when REN renames a group of files you'll get no visual feedback. Above, you're changing the names of all files that end in SYS to end in BRO. Since a wildcard is specified for the filenames, only the extensions change. Pull a directory to confirm this. Type:

```
DIR
```

Press Enter. You'll see all BRO files where once there were SYS. This is a powerful and popular way to rename groups of files with similar extensions.

The files on drive A are really unorganized, which is okay when you consider that it's a demo diskette. But why not clean it up a bit? Let's *move* all the BRO files from the root directory into the BUDGET subdirectory.

- *A "move" involves two steps: COPYing the files to the destination and then DELeting the originals.*

Type in the following:

```
COPY *.BRO \BUDGET
```

Press Enter. This copies all the BRO files to the BUDGET subdirectory. Confirm they're there by typing in:

```
DIR \BUDGET
```

You'll see all the BRO files listed. Now delete the originals to complete the move operation. Carefully type in the following:

```
DEL *.BRO
```

This is a powerful command; when used with wildcards DEL can be most efficient—and potentially fatal. Double check your typing. Press Enter.

DEL is as silent deleting a group of files as it is deleting a single file. All the BRO files are now gone from the root directory. The copies of those files still exist in the BUDGET subdirectory. Remember: A DOS command only affects the files in the current directory.

Confirm that the BRO files are gone from the root. Type in the following:

```
DIR *.BRO
```

The DIR command will only list files matching the wildcard. Press Enter.

```
Volume in drive A is DIRTY
Directory of A:\
File not found
```

Since there are no "*.BRO" files in the root directory, you get a "File not found" message from the DIR command. The files have been successfully moved.

Star-Dot-Star

A special version of the asterisk wildcard is *.*, which DOS users pronounce "star-dot-star." It represents all files in the current directory—all files. As such it's pretty powerful.

Wildcards

Type in the following:

`DIR *.*`

Press Enter.

The DIR command lists all files in the current directory. Of course, that's redundant, since the DIR command does that anyway. So *.* has its best use with the other file manipulation commands.

On drive A, create a new subdirectory DUP. Type in the following:

`MD \DUP`

Press Enter.

Now you're going to copy all files from the root directory to the new DUP directory. Type in the following:

`COPY *.* \DUP`

Carefully check your typing (you're getting into cryptic symbol land). Press Enter.

The COPY command makes a duplicate of each file in the root directory and places it into the DUP subdirectory. Note that only files were copied. The *.* doesn't represent any subdirectories, so COPY didn't copy the BUDGET subdirectory. The *.* wildcard only represents *files* in the current directory.

The Deadly DEL *.*

Carefully type in the following command:

`DEL *.*`

Here you're telling DOS to delete all files in the current subdirectory. With one quick command you can erase thousands of bytes of information. Press Enter. (It's okay.)

`Are you sure (Y/N)?`

Since DEL *.* is so drastic, DOS is confirming that you want to delete all the files in the current directory. Press the N key, then

Enter. You're safely returned to the DOS prompt; no files are deleted.

If you really did want to delete all the files, you'd press Y. DOS is being extra cautious. Yet a few "old hands" quickly type "DEL *.*" and then follow it with Enter and Y. Many a user's day has been ruined by such swiftness. Only use "DEL *.*" if you really need to clean out a directory, and then you should still be careful.

ON USING WILDCARDS

Wildcards can be used by all DOS commands that manipulate files. But keep in mind that a few DOS commands will only work with one file at a time. For example, the TYPE command. Look at the following (don't type it in):

TYPE *.TXT

TYPE only lists the contents of one file at a time. If you entered the above DOS command line (to list the contents of all the TXT files on disk), DOS would tell you, "Invalid filename or file not found"—an error.

Wildcards and Pathnames

Wildcards fit nicely into a pathname. They can be used to represent a group of files in a specific subdirectory on a certain drive. But they cannot be used inside the path. For example, the following line is 100 percent okay:

DIR C:\DOS*.COM

Type in the above command and press Enter.

- *If you get an "Invalid directory" message, then your drive C may not have a DOS subdirectory. Retype the command line using the proper DOS subdirectory name in the path.*

Wildcards

The pathname "C:\DOS*.COM" represents all COM files in your DOS subdirectory. But take a look at this:

C:*\JANUARY*.WKS

The above path is wrong. The asterisk (or question mark) cannot be used to represent a subdirectory in a pathname. It can only be used at the end of a pathname to represent parts of a file.

Limits to the * Wildcard

There is only one oddity with the asterisk wildcard; it only matches one group of characters in a filename. For example:

M*.*

This filename wildcard stands for all files on disk starting with an M and having any filename extension. But consider this:

M.

It seems like the above would match all files whose name ends in M—but that's not the case. Instead, DOS translates it as *.*, all files.

Look at the following filename wildcard:

T*ING

It seems like this would match all files starting with T and ending in ING. Again, that's not the case. DOS translates the above as "T*", which means any file starting with T. If you really want to work with all files starting with T and ending in ING, you use the question mark wildcard:

T????ING

The * wildcard is powerful, just not very smart. Any letters you type after the * (or between the star and the period) are ignored by DOS. It would be nice if it didn't work that way; it would be logical and make sense. But it doesn't.

SUMMARY

DOS uses two types of wildcards, allowing you to work with groups of files at a time. The ? wildcard is used to represent a single character in a filename; the * wildcard represents a group of characters.

These wildcards can be used with the DIR, COPY, DEL and REN commands to manipulate groups of files at a time. As long as the files have some common element in their names, then you can treat them all as a single unit.

A special filename wildcard is *.*, or "star-dot-star." It's used to represent all files in the current directory, or when used with a pathname can represent all files in any subdirectory.

If you'd like to take a break now, feel free to. Turn off your computer by following these steps:

1. Make sure you're at the DOS prompt.
2. Remove any floppy diskettes from the floppy drives (make sure the drive light is off).
3. Turn off all peripherals.
4. Finally, turn off the PC.

Lesson Four

DOS Is Your Slave

CHAPTER 19

Making a Boot Disk

DOS is software that controls your hardware. It's loaded from disk when you first turn on your PC. But how does DOS get there? What magic is necessary to initially install DOS on your PC's hard disk?

Starting with this chapter, you'll be practicing setting up DOS on a floppy diskette. This is what's known as making a *system* or *boot disk*. It's already been done to your hard drive, most likely by someone else. This chapter is where you learn how that was done. But to be safe, you'll be working entirely on a floppy diskette.

If you turned off your PC since the last chapter, follow these steps to turn it on:

1. Turn on all necessary peripherals.
2. Turn on the computer.
3. Enter the date and time.
4. Start working with DOS.

PUTTING DOS ON DISK

There are two ways to make a boot disk:

1. Format the diskette as a *system diskette*.
2. Copy the system to an already formatted disk.

Both of these steps are basically the same. The difference is whether the disk has already been formatted or not. If a diskette is blank, then you use step one: format the diskette as a system diskette. If the diskette has already been formatted, then you use a special DOS command to copy the system to that diskette.

No matter which step you choose, once the system is on a diskette you can use that disk to start the computer.

What Is "The System?"

DOS is a program. It's software that exists on your hard drive and all other "boot disks." It consists of three files, two of which are invisible or "hidden." You'll never see them listed by the DIR command, but they're right there in the root directory. The third file is COMMAND.COM, which you can see in a directory listing. Together, all three of these files form the basic core of DOS—the system.

When you copy those three files on a diskette, it becomes a boot disk. But you can't use the COPY command to copy hidden files. Because of this, you need special DOS commands to make a system diskette. Once that's done, you can use that diskette to start your computer.

MAKING A SYSTEM DISKETTE

To make a boot diskette, first remove any floppy diskettes from your A drive.

Make sure you're logged to drive C, then type:

```
C:
```

and press Enter.

Type the following at the DOS prompt:

```
FORMAT A: /S
```

Check your typing. That's a slash-S, not a backslash. Press Enter.

Making a Boot Disk

```
Insert new diskette for drive A:
and strike ENTER when ready
```

Insert a new diskette in drive A and close the drive door. Press Enter.

Format is now formatting the diskette in drive A—and it's making that diskette a system disk. It's the "/S" switch that tells FORMAT to make a boot disk. When "/S" is specified, the FORMAT command will format the diskette in drive A and then copy the system (DOS) to that diskette. The end result? A bootable diskette.

The formatting will proceed as normal; you'll hear the drive clunking away as it formats each track. But when formatting is done, there will be some extra disk activity. You'll see something like the following displayed:

```
Format complete
System transferred
  1213952 bytes total disk space
    78336 bytes used by system
  1135616 bytes available on disk
Format another (Y/N)?
```

"System transferred" means that the FORMAT command has copied the hidden DOS boot files to that newly formatted diskette. You can also see the number of bytes the system has used on the diskette (78,336 above). Enter a volume label if asked, then press N and Enter to return to DOS.

> ■ *A system diskette has a copy of the DOS boot files on it, the same files that exist on your hard drive. Though DOS says "System transferred," there are still copies of the originals on your hard drive.*

Write on a sticky label "DOS Boot Disk." Then remove the diskette from drive A, peel and stick the label on that diskette. Re-insert the diskette into drive A and close the drive door.

At the DOS prompt, pull a directory of the boot disk in drive A. Type:

```
DIR A:
```

Press Enter. You'll see something similar to the following:

```
Volume in drive A has no label
Directory of A:\
COMMAND COM   25307   3-17-87 12:00p
    1 File(s)    1135616 bytes free
```

In addition to COMMAND.COM, there are two other files on that diskette. They're "invisible" so you don't see them listed. If you're handy at math, you noticed that the size of COMMAND.COM (25,307 bytes) doesn't equal the amount of space FORMAT said was occupied by the system, 78,336.

Testing the Boot Diskette

Make sure the boot diskette works. Keep it in your A drive with the door closed.

You're now going to reset your system. This is done with a special triple-key combination. Press the Control (Ctrl), Alt and Delete (Del) keys all at the same time. Do it now.

Ka-chinka!

Control-Alt-Delete resets your computer. Some PCs have a "Reset" button or switch, which works as well. Either method is a good way to reset the system, as opposed to turning the power off, waiting 15 seconds, then turning it on again.

> ■ *Resetting your computer isn't something you'll be doing all the time. In fact, Control-Alt-Delete truly is a panic switch, used mostly in those types of situations.*

Keep your newly formatted diskette in drive A. (This is one of the rare instances where you will do that.)

After your computer resets, it loads DOS from the newly created DOS diskette in drive A. This way you'll be certain that you've created a true system diskette.

After a time, your boot diskette will be read by the computer,

Making a Boot Disk **169**

and DOS will be loaded into your computer's memory. You'll be asked the date and time, just as described earlier in this book. Type in the current date and time, or press Enter if they're both correct. Soon you'll be at the DOS prompt, logged to drive A.

```
A>
```

Congratulations on making your first DOS boot diskette!

TRANSFERRING THE SYSTEM

If a diskette has already been formatted, you need to use a special DOS command to put the system on it and make it a bootable diskette. That command is SYS. (Don't type this in):

```
SYS A:
```

This command copies the hidden DOS files to the diskette in drive A. After that, you use the COPY command to move over COMMAND.COM. (Again, don't type this in):

```
COPY C:/COMMAND.COM A:
```

When you format a diskette using the "/S" switch, both of these steps are done for you. (This is why you used FORMAT to create your boot disk above.) Therefore the SYS command is used either to put the system on an existing diskette, or to *update* an already-bootable diskette with the latest version of DOS.

You should note that the SYS command doesn't work in all situations. For example, if the diskette in drive A doesn't have room for the hidden files, you'll see a message displayed:

```
No room for system on destination disk
```

In that case, you must start over with another diskette.

SUMMARY

A boot diskette is one that contains the basic DOS files: COMMAND.COM and two hidden files. When the computer starts, it looks for a disk containing those files. Once found, the computer loads DOS from that disk and you're up and running.

Making a boot disk is best done when you first format a disk. By specifying the FORMAT command's "/S" switch, you create a system diskette, complete with COMMAND.COM and the two hidden files. That diskette can then be used to start your computer.

Normally, you just put the system on your hard drive, and it only needs to be done once (when you first set up the computer). If you want to put the system on an already-formatted disk, or update your version of DOS, then the SYS command is used.

Keep your computer on and the boot diskette in drive A for the next chapter.

CHAPTER 20

Customizing DOS With CONFIG.SYS

Your boot diskette in drive A is all you need to start a DOS computer. But starting DOS can involve more than COMMAND.COM and those two hidden files. Two other files, ones which you can create to directly control how DOS works, are the CONFIG.SYS and AUTOEXEC.BAT files.

This chapter is about CONFIG.SYS, which is your system configuration file. Building a good CONFIG.SYS file means your computer will run at top efficiency. Quite a few applications will ask you to modify CONFIG.SYS for the same efficiency reasons, and often when you add new, exotic hardware to your system you'll need to modify CONFIG.SYS as well. It's an important element of using DOS.

ALL ABOUT CONFIG.SYS

CONFIG.SYS is a text file on disk. It contains instructions that tell DOS how to work with your computer, the disk drives, and any other special "devices" you may have added.

When your computer starts, it loads DOS from a boot disk. Part of that loading process involves looking for a file named CONFIG.SYS in the root directory of your boot disk. If found, DOS reads the contents of CONFIG.SYS and carries out whatever instructions you've put there. CONFIG.SYS is used to configure your system.

Looking at CONFIG.SYS

Since CONFIG.SYS is a text file, it's possible to list its contents on the display. That's done with the TYPE command. Type in the following:

```
TYPE C:\CONFIG.SYS
```

Press Enter. You'll see several lines of text displayed on the screen. Those are the contents of your CONFIG.SYS file.

- *If you see a "File not found" error message, then your system doesn't have a CONFIG.SYS file. This is okay: it's optional. But your system runs better with one than without.*

The following shows the contents of a typical CONFIG.SYS file:

```
BUFFERS = 32
FILES = 32
DEVICE = C:\MOUSE\MOUSE.SYS
```

Each line in the CONFIG.SYS file is a command, telling DOS how to configure your system. Because it's "your system," nearly all CONFIG.SYS files are different. For example, one of the above commands loads a "mouse driver," which is software that controls a mouse installed on a PC.

CREATING AND CUSTOMIZING CONFIG.SYS

The purpose behind CONFIG.SYS is to tell DOS about your computer and the way you want to run DOS. Because that information is so definite, modifying CONFIG.SYS isn't done that often; usually once, when you first install DOS, and then again whenever you upgrade or modify your system.

The following two sections describe how to create a new CONFIG.SYS file and then how to change an existing one. The

Customizing DOS With CONFIG.SYS

best tool for doing either operation is a program called a "text editor." That's a special type of word processor that only deals with text files on disk, of which CONFIG.SYS is one.

Building a New CONFIG.SYS File

Just as you created a text file in Chapter 11 using COPY, you'll now use it to create CONFIG.SYS on your boot diskette in drive A. Type the following at the DOS prompt:

```
COPY CON CONFIG.SYS
```

Press Enter.

What you put into your new CONFIG.SYS file is up to you. For practice, I recommend the following two commands as an absolute minimum. Type in the following two lines, pressing Enter after each:

```
BUFFERS = 32
FILES = 32
```

Anything else you place into CONFIG.SYS would depend on individual items in your computer or the software packages you use. But for practice, the above is fine.

- *There are 13 different commands you can place into a CONFIG.SYS file. They're all listed in the DOS manual.*

Press F6 to end the file, then press Enter.

```
1 File(s) copied
```

Changing Your CONFIG.SYS File

Occasionally, you'll install some piece of software or add on some hardware goodie to your PC. When you do, you might be asked to modify your CONFIG.SYS file to reflect the new changes in your system. Sometimes these changes will be made automatically, usually by some sort of INSTALL program. When they aren't, you'll have to edit your CONFIG.SYS file, adding the new changes yourself.

To edit CONFIG.SYS, you have two choices:

- Use a word processor
- Use a text editor

COPY CON is not an option here. Why? Because it doesn't edit files, it only creates them. And with the COPY command, remember that you can copy over an existing file and DOS won't give you a warning. So it's best to use a word processor or text editor, make the changes, and then save CONFIG.SYS back to disk.

Whenever you make changes to CONFIG.SYS, or even when you create a new CONFIG.SYS file, take note of the following:

- *Changes made to CONFIG.SYS only take effect after you reset your computer.*

DOS only reads the commands in CONFIG.SYS once: when the computer boots. So if you modify CONFIG.SYS and want immediate results, save the file to disk, return to the DOS prompt and then reset. (Control-Alt-Delete.)

Don't reset yet! Keep your computer on and running for the next chapter.

SUMMARY

CONFIG.SYS is your system configuration file. It contains commands that configure the way your computer works, the way DOS works, and the way some peripherals (such as a mouse) work. This is all controlled by special commands inside the CONFIG.SYS file.

CONFIG.SYS is a text file, and it's always located in the root directory of your boot disk.

You can list CONFIG.SYS's contents using the TYPE command, and you can create, edit, or update it using a word processor or text editor.

Remember that changes to CONFIG.SYS will only take effect *after* you've reset the computer.

CHAPTER 21

Customizing DOS With AUTOEXEC.BAT

CONFIG.SYS is DOS's basic system configuration file. A second file also allows you to configure DOS. It's AUTOEXEC.BAT—a *batch file*. Batch files are special programs that contain DOS commands. What AUTOEXEC.BAT does is give DOS a bunch of initial setup commands, or run special startup programs, each time you turn on your computer.

This chapter is about AUTOEXEC.BAT and all the fun things you can do with it. First comes a discussion of batch files and how they work. That's followed by a description of AUTOEXEC.BAT and some popular commands you can use in it.

PROGRAM FILES AND BATCH FILES

Program files are just like other files, save for two major differences: A program file contains instructions for the computer, commands that tell it to do something, and all program files have a filename extension of COM, EXE or BAT.

COM and EXE files contain programming instructions that directly tell the computer what to do. But a BAT file is basically a text file. It contains readable text in the form of DOS commands.

Making a Batch File

A batch file is basically a collection of DOS commands—stuff you'd type at the command prompt. In fact, all the DOS commands you've learned so far could be placed into a batch file.

Type the following at the DOS prompt:

```
COPY CON WHAT.BAT
```

Press Enter.

You're now creating the file WHAT.BAT using the keyboard as input. Since this is a text file with a BAT filename extension, DOS will eventually be able to run it as a program (a batch file program). But first, stick some commands in the batch file.

Type the following three lines, pressing Enter after each:

```
CLS
VOL
VER
```

Those are three simple DOS commands: CLS to clear the screen; VOL to display the drive's volume label; and VER to display the DOS version.

To end the file, press the F6 key. Press Enter to finish creating the file.

```
1 File(s) copied
```

Now pull a directory of drive A to look at your work. Type:

```
DIR
```

Press Enter. You'll see something like the following:

```
Volume in drive A has no label
Directory of A:\
COMMAND  COM    25307    8-31-90 10:04a
CONFIG   SYS       26   11-12-92  5:57p
WHAT     BAT       15   11-12-92  6:23p
     3 File(s)   1134592 bytes free
```

Running a Batch File

To run a batch file, or any program under DOS, you only need to type the filename. At the DOS prompt, type:

```
WHAT
```

This tells DOS to locate and run a file named WHAT in the current directory. Press Enter.

Your screen will clear, then you'll see something like the following:

```
A> VOL
Volume in drive A has no label
A> VER
IBM Personal Computer DOS Version 3.30
A>
```

DOS runs a batch file by reading each line of text and then "typing" it at the DOS prompt for you. Everything is automatic; you didn't need to type CLS, then VER, then VOL. Typing "WHAT" at the DOS prompt did it all. Type WHAT again to see the batch file run a second time:

```
WHAT
```

Press Enter.

WHAT.BAT is a valid batch file—a program under DOS. But its contents are trivial. In "real life," a batch file helps you perform repetitive operations by storing a bunch of commonly used DOS commands in a single file. Most DOS users will write batch files to run programs, set up their computers, or perform some task.

ALL ABOUT AUTOEXEC.BAT

AUTOEXEC.BAT is a batch file, like WHAT.BAT you just created. Each time your computer starts, DOS looks for a file named AUTOEXEC.BAT in the root directory of your boot disk. If found, DOS will automatically execute the commands stored in that batch file. It's from that automatic aspect that AUTO-EXEC.BAT gets its name.

Just like the CONFIG.SYS file, AUTOEXEC.BAT is a text file (as are all batch files). It contains DOS commands, plus special batch file commands that set up the way you use your computer.

AUTOEXEC.BAT is optional; you don't need it. But it helps! Without it, DOS will simply ask you for the date and time whenever you start your computer, then you'll see the boring old DOS prompt. If you're clever with AUTOEXEC.BAT, however, you can totally customize the way DOS starts up—even make it a bit friendlier.

Taking a Look at AUTOEXEC.BAT

AUTOEXEC.BAT is always lurking in your boot disk's root directory. To view its contents, use the TYPE command:

```
TYPE C:\AUTOEXEC.BAT
```

Press Enter and you'll see the contents of AUTOEXEC.BAT displayed on your screen.

- *If you saw a "File not found" error, then your system doesn't have an AUTOEXEC.BAT file. That's okay—it's optional.*

Each line of text in your AUTOEXEC.BAT file is a DOS command line, exactly the same as what you'd type at the DOS prompt. There are other, special, batch file "directives" in there as well. But mostly a batch file contains DOS commands and the names of programs.

Creating AUTOEXEC.BAT

Let's create a typical, general, all-purpose, generic AUTOEXEC.BAT file. At the "A>" prompt, type the following:

```
COPY CON AUTOEXEC.BAT
```

Double check your typing, then press Enter.

AUTOEXEC.BAT is a text file, and as such you can create it using COPY CON. (But if you want to edit an existing AUTOEXEC.BAT file, use a text editor or word processor—just as you would with the CONFIG.SYS file.)

Customizing DOS With AUTOEXEC.BAT

Now type in the following lines, pressing Enter after each:

```
@ECHO OFF
DATE
TIME
PROMPT $P$G
PATH C:\DOS
```

To end the file, press the F6 key. Then press Enter to return to the DOS prompt.

```
1 File(s) copied
```

Those are all DOS commands above, each one now a line in the AUTOEXEC.BAT file. Every time your computer starts, it will *execute* each of those five commands.

The only commands you probably recognize above are DATE and TIME. The PROMPT and PATH commands (the last two) are explained in the next chapter. But that first command, "@ECHO OFF," looks more confusing than it really is.

"@ECHO OFF" is used in a batch file to turn off the display while the batch file runs. Normally, when a batch file runs it echoes its commands on the screen. You saw how the commands are echoed when you ran WHAT.BAT earlier. But by putting an "@ECHO OFF" command at the top of a batch file, it runs silently, without displaying text on the screen.

Type in the following:

```
DIR
```

Press Enter. Look for these three files: COMMAND.COM, CONFIG.SYS, and AUTOEXEC.BAT. Those three files are the earmark of a DOS boot disk.

Let's See if it Works

As with CONFIG.SYS, changes made to your AUTO-EXEC.BAT file do not take effect until you reset your computer. So, keep the boot diskette in drive A and reset your computer. Press all three of these keys: Control-Alt-Delete.

Ka-chinka!

Here's what's going to happen: DOS will load from the floppy diskette in drive A. Then DOS will look for *and find* your CONFIG.SYS file. It will configure itself accordingly.

After a time, DOS will look for *and find* your AUTOEXEC.BAT file. It will then execute each line, first asking for the date and time, and then running the mysterious PROMPT and PATH commands. After a time, you'll see:

```
A:\
```

Hey! New prompt! Keep your computer on and running, and you'll find out how that new prompt came into being in the next chapter.

SUMMARY

AUTOEXEC.BAT, like CONFIG.SYS, is a program that helps you set up your computer. But where CONFIG.SYS configured the system, AUTOEXEC.BAT is a batch file that contains a list of DOS commands you always want executed when you first start your computer.

Batch files are text files containing DOS commands. When DOS sees the BAT extension on a file, and you type that file's name at the DOS prompt, DOS will magically type all the commands in the batch file for you. It's a handy way to do many DOS commands at once.

The AUTOEXEC.BAT file on your system contains a list of DOS commands you always want to run when you first start your computer. It must be located in the root directory of your boot disk and, as with CONFIG.SYS, if it's not found DOS will simply assume some things (boring things) about your system, setting it up accordingly.

CHAPTER 22

The PATH and PROMPT Commands

You can really do anything you want in an AUTOEXEC.BAT file, but it's best put to use for system setup and configuration. As you get into using your PC, you may find some special programs you always want to run when the computer starts. If so, then just stick them in as a new line of text in your AUTOEXEC.BAT file.

This chapter continues the exploration of your system's AUTOEXEC.BAT file, concentrating on two commands you saw in the previous chapter: PROMPT and PATH. Of all the DOS commands you can toss into an AUTOEXEC.BAT file, those two are the most popular.

COMMANDS USED IN AUTOEXEC.BAT

Every computer's CONFIG.SYS can be different, customized to that one computer. AUTOEXEC.BAT files are even more diverse. Where CONFIG.SYS has only 13 commands, three of which are popular, the possibilities for an AUTOEXEC.BAT file are limitless. All DOS commands and programs can be put there (though in practice only a few are). Out of that huge possibility, there are two commands you'll find in AUTOEXEC.BAT more than any other: PROMPT and PATH. They're incredibly useful.

Take another look at your AUTOEXEC.BAT file. Type in the following:

```
TYPE AUTOEXEC.BAT
```

Press Enter. You'll see the following:

```
@ECHO OFF
DATE
TIME
PROMPT $P$G
PATH C:\DOS
```

"@ECHO OFF" was explained in the previous chapter. Because it's there, this batch file will not display its DOS commands; you won't see them "typed" for you at the DOS prompt.

The DATE and TIME commands you know. They asked you for the date and time when you first started the computer. (This prompt isn't suppressed by the "@ECHO OFF" command.)

The DATE and TIME commands are rarely put into AUTOEXEC.BAT anymore. Most PCs now come with battery-backed-up clocks that keep track of the date and time automatically. You probably saw the real time and date displayed when prompted, so you just pressed Enter. Because of that, there's really no reason to include DATE or TIME in an AUTOEXEC.BAT file (unless, of course, your PC lacks a clock).

Then you have the PROMPT and PATH commands. They look cryptic and mysterious. But don't let their nature fool you. They're fun and useful commands.

The PROMPT Command

The PROMPT command is used to change the look of your DOS prompt. By default, DOS gives you the standard boring DOS prompt: the drive letter followed by a right angle bracket or "greater-than" sign:

```
C>
```

Yawn!

You can, however, make the DOS prompt look like just about anything, or say anything. Type in the following:

```
PROMPT Your command?
```
Press Enter.
```
Your command?
```
Press Enter a few more times. Type in "CLS" or "DIR" or any DOS command. Yes, that's the DOS prompt. You just modified its look using the PROMPT command.

Carefully type in the following:
```
PROMPT Your wish is$_My command:
```
Note the dollar sign and underline ($_) between "is" and "My" above. Press Enter.
```
Your wish is
My command:
```
The "$_" didn't display. Instead, DOS split the line in two, displaying "Your wish is" on the first line, and "My command" on the next line. Press Enter a few times to see how this prompt looks.

The "$_" is a special PROMPT command. PROMPT uses the dollar sign as a *prefix*. Any character following the dollar sign tells PROMPT to do something special. In this case, "$_" tells PROMPT to produce a new line of text. It allows you to create DOS prompts that use more than one line.

Type in the following:
```
PROMPT $P$G
```
Press Enter.

This is the same PROMPT command you put into your AUTOEXEC.BAT file. There are two special PROMPT commands: "$P" and "$G." The "$P" command causes PROMPT to display the currently logged disk drive and subdirectory—the path. The "$G" command causes PROMPT to display the greater-than sign.

Carefully look over the following and type it in exactly:
```
PROMPT $T$_$D$_$P$G
```

Press Enter.

This PROMPT command uses several special dollar sign commands. The DOS prompt now displays the current time, the current date, the currently logged path, and finally a greater-than sign. It will look something like this:

```
14:55:52.30
Sat 10-31-1992
C:\>
```

That's one informative prompt! Press Enter to assure yourself that the change is real. (Note that the time display doesn't change with the passing time; you must press Enter to see the current time.)

To restore the dull, old, original DOS prompt, you simply type PROMPT by itself. Type in:

```
PROMPT
```

Press Enter. Ho hum.

Most users prefer the type of prompt already in your AUTOEXEC.BAT file. Change the system prompt back to that prompt by typing the following:

```
PROMPT $P$G
```

Press Enter.

The PROMPT command works by changing the prompt to whatever text you place after PROMPT on the command line (or in a batch file). Additionally, there are 13 different prompt commands. Each of them starts with a dollar sign. Some of them display a single character, others display text such as the date or time. A complete list of all the commands is located in Appendix D.

The PATH Command

Another handy command for AUTOEXEC.BAT is the PATH command. But PATH is more of a "behind-the-scenes" command than PROMPT, and in a way, it's more important.

PATH tells DOS where to find program files. Normally, DOS only deals with files in the current directory. Unless a full pathname

The PATH and PROMPT Commands

is specified, DOS won't run any programs outside of the current subdirectory. However, if you install a *search path*, then DOS can locate program files in other subdirectories, as well.

- *A "search path" helps DOS locate program files, forcing DOS to look for them on other drives and in other subdirectories. It will not, however, find non-program files.*

To see your system's current search path, type in the following:

```
PATH
```

Press Enter. By itself, PATH displays the current search path. It may look something like this:

```
PATH=C:\DOS
```

Above, the path is set to the DOS subdirectory on drive C. That means, in addition to looking in the current directory for programs, DOS will also scan C:\DOS, where your DOS files are kept.

Let's assume for a moment that you're using *WordPerfect* and have installed it in the C:\WP subdirectory. If so, you could set a PATH that would find all of *WordPerfect*'s files—even if you aren't currently logged to C:\WP. Type in the following:

```
PATH = C:\DOS;C:\WP
```

See how the second pathname is separated from the first by a semicolon? The semicolon is the path separator character. You can put as many subdirectories "on the path" as will fit, but you must separate each by a semicolon. Press Enter.

The search path is now set to C:\DOS and C:\WP. (Of course, I don't know if you have a C:\WP subdirectory; this is only an exercise.)

Because PATH aids DOS in searching for files, it's one of the best things you can put in an AUTOEXEC.BAT file. In fact, if your system's PATH wasn't set to the DOS subdirectory, you would have never been able to use some of DOS's commands throughout this book.

Unless you specify a PATH, DOS will only look for files in

the current directory. To reset the PATH to nothing, type in the following:

```
PATH
```

That's a semicolon—not a colon—after PATH. Press Enter.

That single semicolon tells DOS to erase the path. Now DOS will only look for files in the current directory. There is no search path! Type in the following:

```
PATH
```

Press Enter.

```
No Path
```

DOS will now only look for programs in the current directory. To prove that, type the following:

```
FORMAT A:
```

Press Enter. (It's okay.)

```
Bad command or file name
```

Since the FORMAT program isn't on drive A, DOS doesn't understand what you typed. Only with a PATH set to the C:\DOS subdirectory will DOS be able to find "FORMAT.COM" and format a disk.

Other Commands

There is a whole plethora (yes, a plethora) of things PC users will stick into their AUTOEXEC.BAT files. The following list describes some of the many things you can do in your AUTO-EXEC.BAT file. As you get into the world of the computer, you may want to try some of these out:

- Set the screen mode
- Set up the printer
- Set a Code Page (for international use/special characters)
- Change the screen color

- Manipulate drives and subdirectories via the SUBST and JOIN commands
- Set environment variables via the SET command
- Run startup programs
- Run application programs or DOS shells

Some AUTOEXEC.BAT programs can get incredibly long and complex. I've seen a few that have just about everything but the kitchen sink in them. This isn't something you need to worry about at this stage in your DOS knowledge. Other books will offer suggestions for AUTOEXEC.BAT, and some of your applications will make changes if needed.

SUMMARY

The AUTOEXEC.BAT file on your system can contain a whole slew (or plethora) of DOS commands you always want to run when you first start your computer. It must be located in the root directory of your boot disk, and as with CONFIG.SYS, if it's not found, DOS will simply assume a few things about your system.

Two important commands worth putting in your AUTO-EXEC.BAT file are the PROMPT and PATH commands.

PROMPT is used to change your system prompt. The new prompt can contain all sorts of text plus special dollar sign commands that display unique symbols or text.

The PATH command sets your system's search path, which is a list of subdirectories in which DOS will look for program files.

You should now remove the DOS boot disk from drive A. Reset your computer (keeping all disks out of the floppy drives). Press Control-Alt-Delete.

CHAPTER 23

Using Applications

Your computer system consists of both hardware and software. Though hardware is often mentioned first, it's the software that's more important. The software controls the hardware, giving it instructions and telling it what to do. Without software, a computer can't really do anything. (The same holds true for a CD player without CDs, or a VCR without videos to play.)

This chapter is about your computer's software, specifically the applications you'll be running on your system. Just playing with DOS gets boring after a while. Using real software is the reason you bought your PC. Since all PC software varies, nothing specific is discussed here. Instead, you'll find a general overview of how software is set up, how it works, and how it works with DOS. From here on, everything you do on your PC depends on the software you run.

How Software Works

"Applications" equals "software" equals "computer programs." They're all the same: programs that run under DOS on your computer (though the term "applications" has a level of prestige associated with it).

Computer applications are all distributed on diskettes. Once you get the diskettes, you make copies of them for everyday use, or you copy information from the originals to your system's hard drive. Then you use the manual that came with the software to decipher how to use the software. Briefly, that's about it.

- *Using the software and being productive with it involves effort on your part, though. Software doesn't make a computer brilliant; it's still your brain that controls what goes on.*

Software comes on diskettes—but the software itself isn't the diskette. Just as a video tape isn't a movie, the software is actually recorded on the disk. From there, it can be read by your computer's disk drives, and then loaded into your computer's memory where it controls the computer and does what it's supposed to do.

Installation

Setting up software is called *installation*. That's a two-step process where you first copy the software from the original diskettes and then *install* the software, customizing it to work in your PC's environment.

Often those two steps are done for you automatically by the program itself. You start installing the program by inserting the first disk (which will be identified by a special label) into your A drive. You then log to drive A and type one of the following (or similar) commands at the DOS prompt:

```
INSTALL
SETUP
RUN
GO
```

The instructions in the manual will tell you exactly what to do. From that point on, the INSTALL (or whatever) program will take over. First it will copy all the files from the distribution diskettes to your hard drive. You may even be asked to shuffle (remove and insert) several diskettes before the operation is over.

After the files have been copied to your hard drive, the INSTALL program will set up and configure the program to work with your computer. You may be asked to identify which computer you have, how much memory it has, the type of printer hooked up, and so on.

- *The INSTALL program will figure out most of this technical information for itself. But some of the "dumb" INSTALL programs will ask you. If you don't know, then call your dealer or refer to your sales slip to see what you have installed.*

COPY A:*.*

Some applications lack INSTALL programs. A good example up until recently was the popular Lotus *1-2-3* spreadsheet program. To set up *1-2-3* you first had to create a subdirectory for it on your hard drive:

```
MD \123
```

That made a *1-2-3* subdirectory, into which you would place *1-2-3*'s files. Next you would insert the *1-2-3* "master" diskette into your A drive and type:

```
COPY A:\*.* C:\123
```

That copied all the files from the master diskette to your *1-2-3* subdirectory. The "COPY A:*.*" operation was repeated for however many diskettes came in the *1-2-3* package.

USING THE APPLICATION

The best way to learn software is to *read the manual*.

Computer manuals take a bad rap. Sure, they're poorly written, often misleading, and show few signs of organization. There's a reason for that: Manuals aren't a high priority. Getting the software done is important. The manual is often an afterthought, assigned to someone with feeble writing skills who doesn't want to write the manual anyway.

Manuals are bad for two reasons: The person writing the manual is too familiar with the subject matter, and the manual is always done way before the software is completed. As a beginner using the program, manuals often aren't any help. But I recommend that you look at them, at least through the "Installation" and "Getting Started" chapters.

The Learning Phase

After installation comes the learning phase. That's usually where you read through several chapters of the manual, or do a *tutorial* on the software. The tutorial is the best way to learn new software. Following step-by-step instructions, you work through exercises that show you what the software can do and how it does it—which is the same approach this book takes with DOS.

Books containing tutorials and additional information on the software package can also be purchased. But beware: Some of those books are shoddy rewrites of the manuals. They won't give you any extra information or offer any hand holding. Read the table of contents and thumb through a few chapters before you buy a tutorial.

Finally, getting to know the software comes with using it. Practice makes perfect. The more you use a program, the better you'll know it. Then, after a time, refer back to the manual to check on anything you may have missed. Often you'll discover some shortcut or new command that will help you get work done faster.

UPGRADING

Software is eternal. A book would be eternal if any author had his way. You keep reading and re-writing, fixing things up, adding new comments, checking a thesaurus for a better word. But eventually the publisher gets mad, so you send off the book, regretting those extra days you could have had to make it that much better.

Software is different. Programmers will always fiddle, making minor adjustments, improving speed and performance, and adding new features. When they do that enough, a new version of your software is announced and released.

Using Applications

If you've filled out your software registration card, the developer will drop you a card in the mail telling you a new version of your software is available and describing how you can *upgrade*. Often that involves paying them money for the new version. But with the new version you'll get new features and more power, so sometimes upgrading is worth it.

Version Numbers

Upgrades to software are earmarked by *version numbers*. All software, including DOS, has version numbers. They tell you which version of the software you're using, which you compare with the "current" version. If your version number is less, then the software developer would like you to upgrade.

DOS's version numbers are good to use as an illustration. For example, DOS (as do all software packages) started out with the initial version 1.0.

- *The "1" is the "major" release number, the "0" the "minor" release number.*

As DOS was improved, "bugs" were found and fixed, and new features were added; a later release, 1.1, was introduced. When enough new items were added or improved, a new version of DOS was introduced, 2.0. This numbering scheme is used by all software; an increase of the major release number denotes major changes, while a minor release number increase denotes only bug fixes and minor improvements.

Consider *WordPerfect*. When I first bought *WordPerfect* it was at version 4.1. That was the fourth major release of *WordPerfect*, the first minor release. Later, version 4.2 came out with some minor improvements. Then, after a long time, the developer announced *WordPerfect* 5.0—a total overhaul of the program.

Do You Really Need to Upgrade?

To upgrade you must pay a fee. I've seen fees range from as little as free to $10 on up through $150. Is it worth it?

Keep this in mind: You don't have to upgrade. If your software is doing the job just fine, then why pay the developer any more money? However, if the new version provides some new feature you think you could use, then consider paying for the upgrade.

Above all, wait. All new versions of software—including DOS—are bound to have some bugs in them. If so, they'll be found by the first few suckers who experience "upgrade fever." When you wait, the developer will catch and fix those bugs. Then you can decide if upgrading is for you.

SUMMARY

This chapter covered the subject of installing, setting up, and running applications under DOS. After all, you bought the computer to run some sort of program. Playing with DOS can be interesting, but it doesn't justify a major purchase like a computer. Applications are what it's all about.

Software comes on diskettes, but it's not the diskette itself. Instead, the software is encoded on the diskette in the form of files. To set those files and programs up to work on your computer, you *install* them. This involves some sort of installation program that copies the files to your hard drive and then sets the program up to work on your personal computer.

Using the application involves working with it. You can read through the manual, try a tutorial, experiment on your own, or buy a book on the subject. The key element here is to work with the software; get to know it and use it for the reasons you bought it. That's when you start becoming productive.

Finally comes the eternal upgrade question: when a new version of the software comes out, should you buy it? The answer is yes, but only if the new version does something you need and you feel the price makes it worth it.

The next chapter wraps up this book, telling you some areas worth looking into for further study.

CHAPTER 24

Related Subjects

Welcome to the wonderful world of DOS. You've received your diploma and are ready to graduate. But before dumping you off into the cruel, cold "real" world, I thought I'd offer you a commencement speech on what you're about to find "out there."

This chapter concludes this book with a discussion of related subjects and areas of further interest you may wish to pursue. This book only takes you so far in your introduction to DOS. The important stuff has been introduced and fully explained. But a lot of material was left uncovered, primarily because it has more to do with becoming a *computer guru* than just a computer operator. If you're interested, the following pages will tell you where to look for more information.

FURTHER DOS STUDY

DOS is one of the most popular subjects for computer books. With 50 million DOS users (at least 75 percent of them confused), there's a great potential market out there.

Each publishing house usually produces three to four DOS titles:

- A beginner's DOS book
- A "using DOS" book

- A DOS reference
- A hard disk management book

Don't let the "beginner's" title fool you; most so-called "beginner's guides" to DOS are just as complex as the intermediate or advanced titles. They do a lot of assuming. The subjects covered in this book would be handled in only two or three quick chapters in those books. So, realistically speaking, you're now ready for the so-called beginner's books after reading this one.

The "Using DOS" books are just as cryptic as the beginning DOS books. (And I don't mean to get nasty, that's just the way it is.) They're often technical, but they do contain quite a few interesting tricks and hints for using DOS.

DOS references are basically rip-offs of the DOS manual. Sometimes you'll find a good DOS reference that really explains how things are done. Often there are useful examples, plus a complete reference for all the DOS commands.

Finally, hard disk management covers the subject of using DOS on a hard drive, plus solving some of the information-management problems hard drive users encounter.

FURTHER SOFTWARE STUDY

If you need more information on the subject of software, then there are plenty of books available. All of the popular software packages have several books written about them. Some are mere re-writes of the manual, but some are good tutorials, with real experts offering hints and suggestions for using the software. Read over these volumes carefully before you pick up something that lacks useful information.

As with the DOS books, you'll often find software books at different levels. The beginner's guides are best for starting out, and advanced titles are usually full of the expert's tricks and hints.

OTHER THINGS YOU MAY FIND INTERESTING

The computer is really an endless well of fun. There is no limit to what you can do with one as long as you keep thinking about it from different angles. Some other areas you may want to look into include the following:

- Technical information

In the old days, all computers were sold with a tech manual. Today, you must purchase them separately. These books will tell you how the computer works and divulge some of its inner secrets. Don't think this information is too advanced; there are plenty of easy-to-understand books on the subject.

- Programming

In the old days, computers were directly equated with programming. But today, no one needs to program a computer in order to use it. Off-the-shelf software allows us to use any computer without knowing a lick of programming. But if you're interested, there are lots of books on programming a computer. (And you don't need to be a math wizard or Vulcan to program a PC.)

- Other esoteric subjects

There's always some nitch of computing that some people find fascinating. Computers can generate music, produce graphics, do animation, play games, talk like human beings, edit video tape, etc. There's even interesting areas such as artificial intelligence, robotics, and simulations. These can all be done on your computer, and there are plenty of books and software packages that will lead the way.

SUMMARY

DOS should no longer be a scary thing to you. The computer is well under your control. But if you desire more information, it's as close as your software or book store.

Computers can do just about anything for anyone. And if you ever run out of things to do with your computer, just visit your local bookshop or software store for some ideas.

I wish you the best of luck with your PC and DOS!

APPENDICES

APPENDIX A

*DOS Command
Cheat Sheet*

Remember: DOS commands can be entered in either upper or lower case text.

DRIVE LOGGING

To log to drive A— **A:**
To log to drive C— **C:**

FORMATTING & VOLUME LABELS

To format a diskette in drive A— **FORMAT A:**
To format and attach a volume label— **FORMAT A: /V**
To change a disk's volume label— **LABEL A:**

DIRECTORY COMMANDS

To display a directory— **DIR**
To display a directory in the "paged" format— **DIR /P**
To display a directory in the "wide" format— **DIR /W**
To display a directory for another drive— **DIR A:**
To display a directory for another directory— **DIR \SUBDIR**
To display the current directory— **CD**
To change directories— **CD \SUBDIR**
To make a new directory— **MD SUBDIR**
To remove a directory— **RD SUBDIR** (it must be empty first)

FILE MANIPULATION COMMANDS

To make a duplicate of a file— **COPY FILE1 FILE2**
To copy a file to another drive— **COPY FILE1 C:**
To copy a file from another drive to the current drive—
COPY C:FILE1
To copy a file to another directory— **COPY FILE1 \SUBDIR**
To copy a file from the keyboard— **COPY CON FILE1**
To delete a file— **DEL FILE1**
To rename a file— **REN OLDNAME NEWNAME**
To list a file's contents— **TYPE FILE1**

MISCELLANEOUS DOS COMMANDS

To clear the screen— **CLS**
To change the date— **DATE**
To change the time— **TIME**
To display the DOS version— **VER**

ERROR MESSAGES

```
File not found
```

Check your typing. DOS can't find the file you specified. You may have forgotten the period, added a space, tacked on an extra period at the end of a file, or used a semicolon or forward slash instead of a colon or backslash.

```
Bad command or filename
```

The DOS command you typed doesn't exist. Check your typing. Also, check your system's PATH to see if the program is located in a subdirectory that isn't currently on the path.

```
Abort, Retry, Fail?
```

Check the diskette in drive A (if applicable). Of the three options, always choose "A."

APPENDIX B

Names

DISK DRIVES AND DEVICES

Disk drives are referred to by their letter, for example:
- Drive A is your first floppy drive
- Drive B is your second floppy drive (if available)
- Drive C is your first hard drive
- Drive D is your second hard drive

Drive C is always the hard drive, even if you lack a B drive.

When referencing a drive in DOS, you use its letter followed by a colon, for example:
- A: refers to drive A
- B: refers to drive B
- C: refers to drive C

These drive letters are actually *devices* under DOS. Other devices are as follows:
- CON refers to your keyboard and display
- PRN refers to your printer
- AUX refers to your serial port

FILENAMES

Here are DOS's rules for naming files:

1. All filenames fit into the 8-dot-3 pattern. You can have filenames of up to eight characters, followed by

an optional dot (period) and up to three additional characters. The first eight characters are referred to as the filename, the last three are the extension.
2. Filenames consist of letters, numbers and symbols.
3. You cannot name a file using the space character or any of the following characters:
 " / \ [ ] : * | + = ; , ? < >

A period may only be used once in a filename to denote the start of the filename extension.

4. A filename can start with any valid character. You cannot start a filename with a dot, space, or any of the above invalid characters.

SUBDIRECTORIES

Subdirectories are storage areas on disk, each containing files. Subdirectories are named just like files, using the 8-dot-3 convention, though users rarely give subdirectories an extension.

PATHNAMES

A pathname gives the specific location of a file in your system. It tells the disk drive, subdirectory, and name of the file. The format for a pathname is:

```
drive:\subdirectory
```

First comes the drive letter, then a colon. That's followed by a backslash to represent the root directory. All other subdirectories follow, each separated by a backslash.

When a filename is included in a path, it's separated from the final subdirectory (its own directory) by a backslash:

```
drive:\subdirectory\subdirectory\
filename.ext
```

APPENDIX C

Special Key Combinations

Here are some special Control-key combinations you can use in DOS:

COMBO	DOES...
Control-C	Cancels a DOS command
Control-H	The same as pressing the Backspace key
Control-I	The same as pressing the Tab key
Control-M	The same as pressing the Enter key
Control-P	Toggles (turns on and off) DOS's Echo-to-printer
Control-Q	Resumes after a Control-S pause
Control-S	Pauses the display (any key to continue)
Control-X	Cancels a line of input (only some DOS versions)
Control-Z	End-of-file marker
Control-[	The same as pressing the Escape (Esc) key

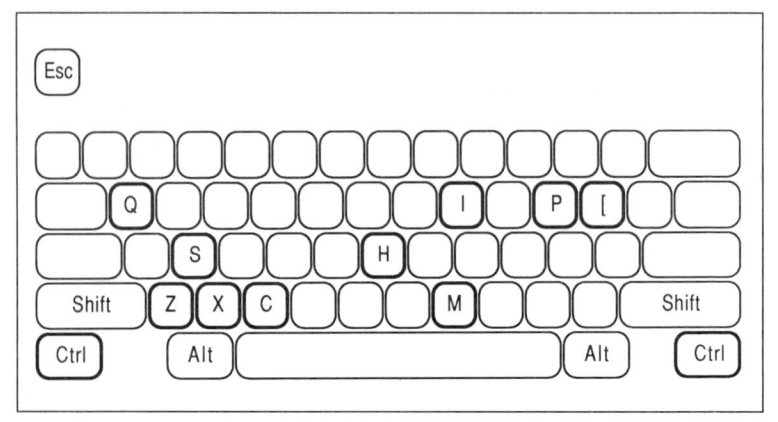

Figure E.1: Control-key combinations.

APPENDIX D

PROMPT Commands

COMMAND	DISPLAYS
$$	$, dollar sign character
$b	| character
$d	the date (according to the system clock)
$e	the ESCape character
$g	>character
$h	backspace (erase previous character)
$l	<character
$n	the logged disk drive letter
$p	the logged disk drive and subdirectory
$q	= character
$t	the current time (according to the system clock)
$v	DOS version
$_	carriage return/line feed (new line)

In addition to these commands, any text appearing after the PROMPT command will appear in your DOS prompt. The most popular DOS prompt is:

```
PROMPT $P$G
```

APPENDIX E

Bits and Bytes

What is a bit? What is a byte? A *bit* is an abbreviation for "*binary digit.*" *Binary* is number base two where there are only two numbers: *one* and *zero*. (Humans work in base 10, where there are ten numbers, zero through nine.) A one or a zero is a binary digit—a bit.

Bits are used with computers because, well, they don't have fingers. Actually, computers are only able to count things that are either "on" or "off." In the case of today's computers, that's the presence or absence of an electrical charge.

The computer groups these bits into *bytes* for practical purposes (easy handling, convenience, interesting puns, etc.). There are eight bits in each byte, eight little switches that can be on or off. And in combination with each other, there are 256 possible arrangements of off-on bits in an eight-bit byte. That's basically how computers count.

Bytes become the basic unit of measurement in a PC. Your RAM, or memory storage, is measured in bytes, and the amount of information stored on a hard drive is measured in bytes.

It's difficult to visualize, say "11 bytes" of something. But consider that you can store one character in a single byte. Or, let's get really simple: one byte is equal to one piece of Alphabits cereal. The letter "A" is a byte. In a computer, you'd need one byte of

RAM to store the letter "A." You'd need eleven bytes to store the word "bellybutton."

As you can imagine, you need a lot of memory (RAM or bytes) to write and store a memo with a word processor. Because of this, RAM is measured in "K"s, rather than individual bytes. One K, or kilobyte, is equal to 1,024 bytes of memory. Again, in layman's terms this would be an entire bowl of Alphabits cereal—without the milk.

- *Why 1,024 and not 1,000? Well, two to the tenth power equals 1,024. Computers like the number two (binary), and 1,024 is the closest power of two to the number 1,000. So there.*

To deal with even larger amounts of memory, "MB"s are used. One MB is a megabyte, which is about one thousand Ks or one million bytes. That's a whole hot tub full of Alphabits cereal.

Technically speaking, one K is equal to 1,024 bytes. One megabyte is equal to 1,024K, or 1,048,576 bytes. Even though that seems like a lot, the typical computer comes with one megabyte of RAM storage, and at least 20 megabytes of hard disk storage. The more the merrier!

APPENDIX F

Tips and Troubleshooting

Here is a checklist you can go over to discover potential problems with your PC:

WHILE BOOTING

- Remove all floppy disks from the disk drives, except boot diskettes.
- Turn on peripherals first, then the system unit—or turn them on together with one master power switch.
- If the computer doesn't boot, check to make sure all cables are connected.
- If you get a "non-DOS disk" error message, check drive A. It may contain a non-boot diskette.
- If the keyboard doesn't work, check the PC's lock (on the front panel of many computers). They keyboard may also be unplugged. If so, turn the computer off before you plug it back in.
- If you see a blank screen, check your monitor. It may be turned off or the brightness may be turned down.
- If you're turning the computer off, wait about 15 seconds before turning it back on again.

212   *Tips and Troubleshooting*

WHILE USING DOS

- Always have plenty of formatted floppy diskettes handy.
- Never remove a diskette from a floppy drive when the drive's light is on.
- The "any key" is either the spacebar or Enter key.
- Press Control-C or Control-Break to cancel a DOS command.
- Press Control-S to pause the display, any other key to resume.
- Remember to turn on the printer before you try printing something.
- If DOS's Echo-to-printer is on, press Control-P to cancel it.
- Do not format your hard drive.
- Control-Alt-Delete is used to reset your computer.

WHILE USING SOFTWARE

- Put write-protect tabs on new software disks before you install or copy the software to your hard drive.
- Occasionally save what you're doing, or use an application's automatic backup feature.
- Exit or quit from a program and return to DOS when you're done.
- Do not shut off the computer to end an application
- Do not reset the computer while an application is running
- Okay, you can stop or reset while an application is running, only if you have no other control over the computer. (It's run amok!)

Tips and Troubleshooting *213*

DURING SHUTDOWN

- Properly exit or quit any applications before turning off the PC.
- Wait until all disk activity stops (no drive lights are on).
- Turn off the power.
- Wait at least 15 seconds before turning the computer on again.

FLOPPY DISK CARE AND HANDLING

- Always pick up a diskette by its edges.
- Keep the diskette away from magnets, such as the secret ones in your phone handset.
- Don't leave a diskette in the sun.
- Don't touch the magnetic surface of a diskette.
- Keep 5¼-inch diskettes in their protective sleeve when not in use
- Label your diskettes! But write on the label *before* peeling and sticking it on the diskette.
- Don't pinch or fold diskettes, or paperclip them.
- Don't get a diskette wet.
- Diskettes have a life span of about six years. If you use one every day, it may last six months. The point is: diskettes are temporary.

COMPUTER CARE AND HANDLING

- Keep your computer out of the sun.
- Keep your computer in a well-ventilated place. Don't keep it butt-against a wall. It needs to breathe.
- Avoid spilling liquids in your PC.

- Do not smoke around a computer. (Smokers will ignore this one, but non-smokers should shoo smokers away at all times.)

SOME SUPPLIES YOU MAY NEED

[ ] Box of diskettes
[ ] Printer paper
[ ] Printer ribbons
[ ] Documentation (books, manuals, etc.)

Index

Index

8-dot-3, 103, 122
  See also filenames
@ECHO OFF, 179

A

Any key, 34
applications, 189
  See also software
  use of, 191
AUTOEXEC.BAT, 175
  commands, 181
  creating, 178

B

Backslash key, 28, 124, 128
Backspace key, 15
batch files, 175
binary digit, 209
  See also bit
bit, 209
boot disk, 4, 165
  testing, 168
booting, 4
  potential problems, 211
  See also powering up
byte, 209

C

child, 129
cleanup, 108
command format, 73
command prompt, 9
  See also DOS prompt
commands
  See DOS commands
CONFIG.SYS, 171
  creating, 172
  editing, 173
Control-Alt-Delete, 34
  See also Reset
Control-Break, 33
Control-key
  combinations, 205
Control-P, 150
Control-Q, 33
Control-S, 33, 146
Control-Z, 92
COPY, 89
  destination, 98
  overwriting, 101
  source, 98
cursor, 14
cursor control keys, 28, 30
cursor key controls, 30
cylinder, 66
  See also formatting

D

data files, 49
default, 83
destination, 98
devices, 92
  CON, 92
  drives, 203
directory
  entries, 117
  printing, 148
disk drives, 53
  location, 54
  sizes, 56
diskettes
  care, 59
  density, 57
  parts of, 58
  removal of, 60
  sticky labels, 61
  use of, 58
DOS, 3
  getting started, 3
  tips, 212
DOS command line, 15
DOS commands, 19
  @ECHO OFF, 179
  Abort, Retry, Fail, 71

CD/CHDIR, 123, 129
cheat sheet, 201
CLS, 20
COPY, 90, 97
DATE, 22
DEL, 107
DIR, 39, 69, 95, 143
directory, 201
Echo-to-printer, 150
ERASE, 108
file manipulation, 202
FORMAT, 65
LABEL, 76
MD/MKDIR, 120
miscellaneous, 202
PATH, 181
PROMPT, 181, 207
REN/RENAME, 105
TIME, 22
TYPE, 47, 95
VER, 24
VOL, 24, 71, 74
DOS prompt, 13
See also command prompt
DOS shells, 142
DOS, defined, 38
dot, 130
double density, 57
See also floppy drives
double dot, 130
drive door, 60
drive light, 60

E

eject button, 60
Enter key, 15
error messages, 202
Escape key, 17
extentions, 51
See also filenames

F

F-keys, 28
See also function keys
F6 key, 92
file list, 145
file management, 89, 105
wildcards, 157
filenames, 42, 103, 203
8-dot-3, 103
extentions, 51
valid/invalid, 103
wildcards, 153
files, 38
AUTOEXEC.BAT, 50
batch, 175
COMMAND.COM, 48
CONFIG.SYS, 50, 171
copying, 97
creating, 90
data files, 49
deleting, 107
locating, 144
management, 89, 105
naming, 103, 138
organizing, 116
program files, 49
renaming, 105
text files, 49, 93
floppy disk
care, 213
floppy drives, 53
capacities, 57
densities, 57
sizes, 56
FORMAT
hard drive warning, 68
options, 73
formatting, 63
cylinder, 66
explanation of, 64
head, 66
sectors, 65

Index

tracks, 65
function keys, 28, 29

G
general failure, 70

H
head, 66
  See also formatting
high density, 57
  See also floppy drives
Hold key, 33
  See also Pause

I
INSTALL, 191

K
keyboard, 27
  backslash key, 28, 124, 128
  Backspace key, 15
  Caps Lock, 31
  cursor control keys, 30
  Enter key, 15
  Escape key, 17
  F-keys, 28
  Hold key, 33
  modifier keys, 28
  Num Lock, 32
  numeric keypad, 30
  Print Screen key, 33
  Scroll Lock, 32
  soft keys, 28
  state keys, 31
  text editing keys, 30
kilobyte, 56

L
laptop, 28
logged to, 14
logging, 79
  Drive A, 80
  Drive B, 81
  logical drive, 81
  physical drive, 81
  subdirectories, 123
logical drive, 81
Lotus *1-2-3*, 51

M
megabyte, 56
modifier keys, 28
  Alt, 28
  control (Ctrl), 28
  Shift, 28

N
names
  drives, 203
  filenames, 203
  pathnames, 204
  subdirectories, 204
numeric keypad, 28, 30
  See also keyboard

O
overwrite, 101

P
parameters, 48, 73
parent, 129
pathnames, 128, 134, 204
  backslash, 128
  wildcards, 160
Pause, 33
pausing, 145
peripheral controller, 5
perspective, 110
physical drive, 81
powering up, 3, 89
  See also booting
Print Screen key, 33, 148
program files, 49

R

read/write head, 53
Reset, 168
root directory, 118, 130

S

screen dump, 33
   See also Print Screen
sectors, 65
   See also formatting
self-test, 5
shift-lock, 31
   See also state keys
shutdown, 213
soft keys, 28
   See also function keys
software, 189
   See also applications
   care, 212
   installation, 190
   reference, 196
   source, 98
   star-dot-star, 158
   See also wildcards
state keys, 31
   Caps Lock, 31
   Num Lock, 31
   Scroll Lock, 31
sticky labels, 61, 67, 76
subdirectories, 115
   copying, 134
   creating, 118
   file management, 133
   limitations, 141
   logging, 123
   naming, 122
   organization, 127
   removing, 140
supplies, 214
system diskette, 165
   See also boot disk
system transfer, 169

T

text editing keys, 30
   See also cursor control keys
text files, 49, 93
toggle, 150
tracks, 65
   See also formatting
tree structure, 130
troubleshooting, 211
tutorial, 192
typematic, 16

U

upgrading, 192
   version numbers, 193
utilities, 142

V

version numbers, 193

W

wildcards, 153
   limitations, 161
   question mark, 154
   star, 155
   use of, 160
write protection, 61
   notch, 61
   tab, 61
   tiles, 61

Other books from
Computer Publishing Enterprises:

Parent's Guide to Educational Software and Computers
by Lynn Stewart and Toni Michael

How to Understand and Find Software
by Wally Wang

How to Get Started With Modems
by Jim Kimble

How to Get Started in Desktop Publishing
by the *ComputorEdge* Staff

Ten (& More) Interesting Uses for Your Home Computer
by Tina Berke

Simple Computer Maintenance and Repair
by Wallly Wang and Scott Millard

101 Computer Business Ideas
by Wally Wang

How to Make Money With Computers
by Jack Dunning

Computer Entrepreneurs
People Who Built Successful Businesses Around Computers
by Linda Murphy

The Best FREE Time-Saving Utilities for the PC
by Wally Wang

The Official Computer Widow's (and Widower's) Handbook
by Experts on Computer Widow/Widowerhood

The Computer Gamer's Bible
by R. Andrew Rathbone

Digital Dave's Computer Tips and Secrets
by Roy Davis

Beginner's Guide to DOS
by Dan Gookin

DOS Secrets
by Dan Gookin

To order these books in the United States or Canada, call 1-800-544-5541.